HOW TO
MAKE YOUR NET WORK
TYING RELATIONAL KNOTS FOR GLOBAL IMPACT

HOW TO
MAKE YOUR NET WORK
TYING RELATIONAL KNOTS FOR GLOBAL IMPACT

by

Dr. James O. Davis

Cutting Edge International
Orlando, Florida

Over the last thirty years, I have been fortunate to give more than 10,000 life-saving presentations and meet tens of thousands of people. Yet, when I met Gary and Lila Stambaugh and saw their deep devotion to Christ and their broad vision for the world, I knew instantly that I was standing with two of the greatest Christians of the twenty-first century.

Due to the amazing generosity of Gary and Lila Stambaugh, *How to Make Your Net Work* became a reality for the global Church!

What Leaders Are Saying About
How to Make Your Net Work

It has been my joy to be involved in the Billion Soul Network from its conception. In my opinion, James O. Davis, one of the leading networkers of our time, has provided a successful roadmap for us to follow. Read *How to Make Your Net Work* today!

~ Jack Hayford
President, The King's University

I don't know of anyone more interconnected than James O. Davis in the global Church. The Lord has equipped him with the leadership ability to tie relational knots like very few leaders of our generation. *How to Make Your Net Work* will powerfully impact the life of everyone who reads it.

~ George O. Wood
General Superintendent, Assemblies of God

It has been our joy to network with the Billion Soul Network. James O. Davis has taken networking to an entire new level in this generation! Your world view will change, your decisions will be more well-rounded, and your mind will be expanded like never before through *How to Make Your Net Work*.

~ Mark L. Williams
General Overseer, Church of God, Cleveland, TN

Every Kingdom-minded leader ought to read *How to Make Your Net Work*. It is destined to become a global networking resource for the Church. This single volume will help you to go from to learning how to network to linking for maximum impact.

~ Stan Toler
General Superintendent, Church of the Nazarene

I don't know of a more defining book for the Church right now. *How to Make Your Net Work* is a must read for every key leader who seeks his/her role in God's goal in the world today.

~ **Fred Luter**
President, Southern Baptist Convention

Foursquare International has globally benefited from the networking leadership of James O. Davis. *How to Make Your Net Work* will teach you how to tie relational knots for the greatest harvest ever in your life and ministry. Read it now and reap for years to come!

~ **Glenn Burris**
President, Foursquare International

The Lord gifted James O. Davis with the divine, unique ability to network throughout the global Church for Kingdom advancement. *How to Make Your Net Work* is the capstone of decades of work. It is destined to become a bestseller!

~ **Doug Beacham**
Presiding Bishop, International Pentecostal Holiness Church

In an era when seemingly there is so much tug-of-war between various Christian organizations, James O. Davis, in *How to Make Your Net Work*, shows us how to pull together instead of pulling apart to achieve greater outcomes than ever before. I champion the global cause of this book and challenge you to secure your copy now.

~ **Frank Damazio**
Chairman, Ministers Fellowship International

I have seen firsthand the networking ability of James O. Davis. I have often said that James knows how to make the net work. After ten years of building the strongest and largest pastors network on the globe, he has now chosen to reveal his secrets of success. Read it and get ahead of the curve before it is too late!

~ **Leonard Sweet**
Best Selling Author & Futurist, E. Stanley Jones Professor of Evangelism

Growing up on the California coast, I have always been in awe of the massive redwood trees, whose unseen strength is found in the knotting of their roots together beneath the surface. I am thrilled that James Davis is teaching us as leaders and followers of Christ how to tie deep knots that will enable us to grow taller and stronger than ever. The height of your life will always depend on the depth and connectedness of your roots.

~ **Paul Louis Cole**
President, Christian Men's Network

How to Make Your Net Work will show you how to connect global thinkers into your life for the achievement of a goal greater than you have imagined. You will learn to see ahead of the visionary curve and make the adjustments necessary to grow your organization in an interconnected world. Both powerful and prophetic, James O. Davis teaches us the reproductive steps of networking in our lives.

~ **Kenneth C. Ulmer**
Senior Pastor, Faithful Central Bible Church

James O. Davis is the leading thinker of global networking in the Body of Christ today. I have seen him turn various streams of Christianity into a mighty river of evangelism. Every Christian leader will greatly benefit from reading *How to Make Your Net Work* and applying its principles to their personal and professional lives.

~ **Sharon Daugherty**
Senior Pastor, Victory Christian Center

I am thrilled with the global release of *How to Make Your Net Work*. If we are ever going to complete the Great Commission in any future generation, it will be the result of a biblically balanced networking approach that releases synergistic outcomes. *How to Make Your Net Work* is that kind of resource. James O. Davis went out to build a global net that works first and now has now has come back to tell us how to do it.

~ **Ronnie Floyd**
Senior Pastor, Cross Church

My friend James Davis travels more extensively, speaks in more venues, and engages more people in meaningful interaction than almost anyone I know. His entire life is built around networking—and his nets work! This man knows whereof he speaks! No one is better equipped or able to write on this topic than this networker himself. *How to Make Your Net Work* will enhance your ability to build meaningful relationships and your passion to do so.

~ **James Merritt**
Founding Pastor, Crosspointe Community Church
Former President, Southern Baptist Convention

James O. Davis is providing excellent visionary networking throughout the Body of Christ. I have witnessed and experienced this firsthand at our church and among key Church leaders from all over the world. In his latest book *How to Make Your Net Work*, he reveals the principles and also the practical steps to unleash local and global synergies for fulfillment of the Great Commission.

~ **Mark Balmer**
Senior Pastor, Calvary Chapel Melbourne

I have heard James O. Davis repeatedly say, "In the future, those who are not networking will not be working." I do not know of anyone more qualified to write a book entitled *How to Make Your Net Work* than him. You will learn how to build a globally networked organization with measurable outcomes larger than you ever imagined possible.

~ **Leon Fontaine**
Founding Pastor, Springs Church, Canada

I have watched James O. Davis traverse the planet interconnecting strategic relationships to help double the size of the global Church. After more than ten years of synergistic leadership, James has chosen to release *How to Make Your Net Work* for the entire Body of Christ. This powerful book will equip, enlighten, and empower you to fulfill your visionary destiny.

~ **Brian Houston**
Senior Pastor, Hillsong Church, Australia

How to Make Your Net Work is a must resource for this generation. With the exploding of global population, combined with financial earthquakes, James O. Davis has provided just the book to compel us to refocus on what matters the most and recommit to add compounding value to each other. He teaches and illustrates the steps to success for making your net work in your life.

~ **Jim Garlow**
Senior Pastor, Skyline Church

Dr. James O. Davis has been my Minister of Networking for over a decade. He has helped me greatly in my journey to amalgamate a fractured group of doctors from all over the world to create a unified wellness movement. As he teaches in *How to Make Your Net Work*, we can do more together than we can do by ourselves.

~ **Ben Lerner**
Founder, Maximized Living Inc.

James O. Davis understands networking! Our Lord has used him to tie powerful, harvesting knots throughout the Body of Christ. In his latest book, *How To Make Your Net Work,* you will learn firsthand the principles that he has practiced in more than one-hundred nations. Be sure to secure your copy today!

~ **Reinhard Bonnke**
Founder, Christ For All Nations

I have known James O. Davis for twenty-five years. Over the years, I have observed him diligently build a worldwide network of pastors to fulfill the task of the Great Commission. *How to Make Your Net Work* is a book that has been forged from a leader who has personally experienced how God turns challenges into opportunities. I highly recommend this book to every Great Commission leader!

~ **Prince Guneratnam**
Senior Pastor, Calvary Church, Malaysia

James O. Davis has provided a remarkable book, *How to Make Your Net Work*. You will be a much wiser, Kingdom-minded leader after you have digested this powerful book and applied its principles to your life. Get it today and benefit for a lifetime!

~ **Eddy Leo**
Senior Pastor, Abba Ministries, Indonesia

James O. Davis inspired me to build a global networked church in my lifetime. Over the years he has taught us how to network through his leadership example in the Body of Christ. *How to Make Your Net Work* combines his experience and knowledge into one dynamic book. Your faith will be increased to believe our Lord for greater results in the years to come.

~ **Suliasi Kurulo**
Founding Pastor, World Harvest Center, Fiji

How to Make Your Net Work is born out of the proven results of James O. Davis, as he has crisscrossed the globe tying strong relational knots for Kingdom advancement. You will be both inspired and instructed by a leader whose ultimate goal is help us all to finish the Great Commission together!

~ **Peter Mortlock**
Founding Pastor, City Impact Church, New Zealand

You should purchase your copy of *How to Make Your Net Work* as soon as possible. James O. Davis reminds us that if our personal goals do not include every person on the planet, ours is not a God-sized vision. He teaches us how to birth, build, balance, and broaden a net that works in any cultural context and results in nets filled with the largest harvest possible.

~ **David Mohan**
Founding Pastor, New Life Assembly, India

In *How to Make Your Net Work*, James O. Davis reveals time-proven strategic principles for forging and building visionary and effectual partnerships that will synergize the Majority World churches and Western churches to the next level of global evangelism, discipleship, and church planting. As principles outlined in this book are implemented and realized, it is well within the universal church's God-given enablement to complete the Great Commission in our lifetime.

~ **James Hudson Taylor IV**
Global Liaison, Overseas Missionary Fellowship, Taiwan

For nearly ten years, James O. Davis and I have served together in many different events and locations for the cause of Christ. Even though we have come from different streams of Christianity, we have learned how to add compounding value to each other. *How to Make Your Net Work* will be a game-changing book for everyone who reads it. You will come to know immediately that the author has lived out what he is now teaching the global Church.

~ **Ademola Ishola**
General Secretary, Emeritus
Nigerian Baptist Convention, Nigeria

Every time we have hosted James O. Davis in East Africa, his teaching has helped to make our network stronger! His book *How to Make Your Net Work* will equip you just as his teaching has empowered us. In the last five years, thousands of churches have been planted in our region, as we have learned how to synergize together. You will find this book hard to put down once you have begun to read it!

~ **Alex Mitala**
Chairman, New Birth Fellowship, Uganda

I have been involved in the Billion Soul Network from the first day of conception and launch more than ten years ago. James O. Davis listened and learned from more than 10,000 key leaders face-to-face before he chose to write *How to Make Your Net Work*. You will come to know what I have seen firsthand: James is the most qualified person today to write on this theme. Learn and link like never before!

~ **David Sobrepena**
Founding Pastor, Word of Hope, Philippines

James O Davis is a master at networking. The secrets to his global success are revealed in this timeless book entitled *How to Make Your Net Work*. He has mastered the principles of moving from collaborator to connector and the Billion Soul Network is living proof. This book will excite any heart that desires to learn networking as a strategy to fulfilling the Great Commission.

~ **Michael Knight**
Founder, The Never Before Project

How to Make Your Net Work: Tying Relational Knots for Global Impact

Copyright © 2013 James O. Davis

James O. Davis
P. O. Box 411605
Melbourne, FL 32941-1605

www.JamesODavis.com
www.billion.tv

DEDICATION

This book is dedicated to visionary Christian leaders throughout the global Church who have chosen to synergistically network to achieve strategic global impact among the 2.4 billion people who have NEVER heard the gospel!

CONTENTS

FOREWORD

At the close of 2011, the earth's population was estimated by the United States Census Bureau to be more than 6.9 billion. The world population has been growing continuously since the end of the Black Death around 1400. The fastest rates of world population growth (above 1.8 percent) were seen briefly during the 1950s, then for a longer period during the 1960s and 1970s.

According to population projections, world population will continue to grow until at least 2050. World births have leveled off at about 134 million per year since their peak at 163 million in the late 1990s, and they are expected to remain constant. However, deaths are only around 57 million per year and are expected to increase to 90 million by the year 2050. Because births outnumber deaths, the world's population is expected to reach about 9 billion by the year 2040.

While the earth's population continues to compound numerically, global Christianity is also growing faster today than at any other time in history. These are unprecedented days of global growth, marked by untold millions of people coming to Christ. A few examples will no doubt convince you of this unparalleled growth of global Christianity. There are more than 120 million Christians in China. There are more Christians in China than members of the Communist Party. Indonesia, with the largest Muslim population in the world, has now become 30 percent Christian. By 2050 the African continent will become a Christian continent with more than one billion Christians. More than 300,000 churches have been planted in Latin America in the last fifty years. South Korea has become the second largest missionary-sending nation in the world, following the United States. Missionaries are now coming to North America from every world region.

We are witnessing an enormous, international missional shift, even greater than the Protestant Reformation. I have heard Dr. James O. Davis, the cofounder of the Billion Soul Network, often say, "We are moving from the 'West going to the Rest' to the 'Best going to the Rest.'" The new missional mantra of the twenty-first century is "Everyone everywhere." The essence of the Billion Soul story demonstrates first-hand the rise of global Christianity as the most powerful, influential force throughout the world.

When the late Dr. Jerry Falwell and I founded Liberty University in 1971, the initial God-given vision was to build a Christian university with 50,000 students, to equip them and send them out to every nation. Even though Dr. Falwell has graduated to eternity, I am grateful that Liberty University today has more than 50,000 students and has become the largest Christian university in the world. It was a bold vision in 1971 to announce a goal of 50,000 students at one university; but today we are approaching more than 100,000 students worldwide.

How to Make Your Net Work is about a faith-filled, bold vision of key Christian leaders—from more than 1,450 unique denominations/organizations and every world region—committed to synergizing their efforts and expertise together to accomplish a goal that is not achievable alone: planting five million new churches for a billion soul harvest in this generation! As you embark on the journey of reading this remarkable book, you will soon discover new worlds that you did not know existed in the landscape of the global Church. *How to Make Your Net Work* is about:

- *Synergizing* leadership efforts to help fulfill the Great Commission
- *Seeking* God's face for the supernatural to become commonplace throughout the world.

- *Saving* the unreached, unsaved and unchurched until all know Jesus as Savior in their language
- *Sending* disciples to advance the Kingdom of God
- *Sharing* resources so pastors and leaders might be equipped to fulfill their calling in every community on earth
- *Sowing* financially for the greatest harvest in history

Dr. James O. Davis and I have been friends for nearly twenty years. I have watched him lead and labor as he has helped to build the Billion Soul Network into the largest pastors' network in the world, one saved person at a time. I have been afforded the opportunity to travel and minister with him in different world regions and have witnessed up-close general overseers, district superintendents, leading pastors, missionaries, and college presidents making strategic commitments to share their resources to plant churches where the Gospel has never been heard before. I do not know of another Christian leader anywhere who has the ability to network the Body of Christ together like Dr. Davis in this generation.

How to Make Your Net Work is about ordinary people achieving extraordinary results. It is a thrilling story about those who have little resources accomplishing much, in a time when those who have much are too often achieving little. As you read these pages, you will be inspired to believe God for great things in your life. You will be instructed how to accomplish these same enormous outcomes. After reading *How to Make Your Net Work,* you will never be satisfied with an average ministry life again.

~ Dr. Elmer Towns
Cofounder, Liberty University
August 2012

INTRODUCTION

I remember as if it were just yesterday. On October 19, 2002, we were celebrating Dr. Bill Bright's eightieth birthday at the Orlando Airport Hyatt in Orlando, Florida. Dr. Bright was the Founder of Campus Crusade for Christ. He passed away less than a year later, on July 19, 2003. But on that day in October 2002, key Christian leaders from around the world had gathered in Orlando, and we were having a wonderful time together celebrating Dr. Bright's milestone day.

The late Dr. Adrian Rogers, former Senior Pastor of Bellevue Baptist Church in Memphis, Tennessee, brought a dynamic presentation about the value of evangelism, discipleship, and the Great Commission. Then, in the middle of his message, he paused and asked a question I will never forget.

"Have you ever thought about what a net is, and what it does?" he asked. "A net is a lot of little strings tied together. Unless you have the tying of those strings together, you won't have a net. You can't catch much with one little string, but you can catch a lot with a net."

Then he looked around the room and into the faces of each of the gathered leaders. "We are a lot of little strings tied together," he said. "That's what makes the net work."

This illustration, so simple yet profound, sharpened the focus of my ministry from that day forward. The essence of networking is the tying of relationships for a greater cause. Without knowing how to tie relationships together and cultivate them, you will never be able to make a net work in your life, your ministry, or your organization.

Perhaps the first association that comes to your mind when you hear the word *network* is *television network.* I grew up in an era when there were only three television networks: ABC, CBS, and NBC. To this day, each one still calls itself a network. For example, the American Broadcasting Company owns a series of affiliate stations throughout the United States and the world. The "network" is actually a chain of linear connections with ABC programming moving along ABC passageways to ABC stations. There is no *inter-*networking and no *inter-*connectivity with sources outside ABC.

The first recorded description of the way social interactions could be enabled and enhanced through a more multi-layered networking concept was in a series of memos written by J.C.R. Licklider of the Massachusetts Institute of Technology. In August 1962, while discussing his Galactic Network concept, Licklider envisioned a globally-interconnected set of computers through which everyone could quickly access data and programs from any site. In spirit, the concept was very much like the Internet of today.

Without knowing how to tie relationships
together and cultivate them, you will never be able
to make a net work.

When I think about a network among Christian leaders, I don't think about a linear network. I think about something that is much more diverse, interconnected, global, and relational—something closer to Licklider than ABC. I think about cross-networking, cross-pollinating, cross-cultural interacting. I think about different and distinct individuals, ministries, and organizations adding synergistic value to one another—like ABC, CBS, and NBC sharing the best of their personnel, resources, programming, and ideas (as if that would ever happen!)

In this book I want to describe and define what a network is in the Body of Christ and how a vibrant one can function for you and your organization. Let's begin, however, by thinking about why is it that so many well-meaning Christians—believers who know they are compelled, commissioned, and called to make disciples for the fulfillment of the Great Commission—refuse to network with others outside their own denominational or organizational tribe. Why do so many local pastors, whether in large metropolitan areas or in remote areas of the world, choose to operate like ABC, NBC, and CBS rather than network together for the noble and higher Great Commission cause? Is it because they do not fully understand the Great Commission and its scope? Why do leaders of major Christian organizations refuse to develop long-term networking relationships with one another? Is it because of doctrinal distinctives or prejudices?

Think about this for a moment: We have a divine mandate from the King of the universe to go out and fulfill the Great Commission—yet we who are leaders in the Church and brothers and sisters in Christ are not willing to working together to make it happen!

In many ways, this book is a how-to book. It is not written simply to teach how to birth, build, and broaden a network among believers. It is also written to answer these two fundamental questions: Why are most Christian leaders not willing to network together? What can be done to change their minds and hearts for the advancement of the Kingdom and the glory of God?

The fact is, if we're ever going to fulfill the Great Commission and reach the whole world for Christ, temporary links will never be enough. We need to be tied together. We need strong, thick *knots*. We need local, regional and global interconnected knots that pull the global Church together into an harmonious net for the greatest harvest of all time!

I'm reminded of the familiar story in Luke chapter 5, where Peter and a handful of disciples had been fishing all night but hadn't caught a single fish. Perhaps you, like me, have felt that way at times: you have been working hard at your ministry but are catching nothing. It is probably not an exaggeration to say that most ministers today are more busy than they are successful.

Is this the way that ministry is supposed to be? Are we called to commit ourselves without a catch? To work all night and go home with an empty boat? To put in our best years—the best of our energy, time, and focus—and not catch much, if anything at all?

Peter had been working hard, with no results. Then Jesus got into the boat. "Put out into the deep water," He said to Peter, "and let down your nets for a catch" (Lk. 5:4).

These words no doubt sounded ridiculous to Peter, as they would to most of us. The sad truth is, too many Christian leaders have either lost or chosen to ignore the liberating truth behind this command of our Lord.

I can imagine what was going through Peter's mind: *But Lord, I have been working as hard as I can! I am a seasoned fisherman. This is my trade. I know what I am doing. I promise You, there's nothing out there!*

Thankfully, Peter didn't stop with his doubts. "Master, we have worked hard all night and caught nothing," he said, "but I will do as You say and let down the nets" (Lk. 5:5).

I'm sure you know the rest of the story. The nets were cast and a great harvest of fish was pulled in. In fact, the catch was so great, Peter's nets began to break. The fish were so plentiful, he was on the verge of losing the entire harvest! That's when the real urgency set in. A crisis was building before his eyes. If Peter didn't do something fast, the catch would be gone in a matter of moments, lost forever.

Who wouldn't want to have a harvest like that? I want this kind of harvest in all ministry, for every one of us—where the nets are so full, they are bulging and beginning to break. I want so many people coming to Christ that it forces us to figure out a solution for getting all of them into the Kingdom while there is still time.

What did Peter do? Did he let his nets break and risk losing the fish? Did he try to take care of the matter all by himself? No. He called out to the fishermen in another boat and urged them to hurry over to help him catch the fish and get them into their boat too, before it was too late.

In many places on the planet today, there are so many people coming to Christ that the Church must work together in order to get the harvest in before it is too late.

This is the essence, the significance, of making the net work. The question is, can the Lord trust us with the size of the catch or will we allow the harvest to be lost?

Jesus trusted Peter with nets that were bulging with fish because He knew Peter was willing to share the catch. Other fishermen may not have worked as long or as hard as Peter had but Peter was willing to share the massive catch with them rather than watch it fall back into the sea.

I submit to you that one of the greatest, if not *the* greatest, problem today in the Church—particularly the Western Church—is that pastors and leaders are wrapped up in their own personal ministries rather than in the Lord's ministry. As a result, they're more willing to lose the harvest than to share it. Of course, whenever we talk about why Christian leaders refuse to work together, the conversation usually centers around doctrinal issues or the uniquenesses we have in Christ. We talk about our different backgrounds, cultures and ethnic groups. Yet, the bottom line, the unspoken reason, is really this: Pastors and leaders do not work together because they are not willing to share the catch. They don't like the idea that a new convert may end up in another pastor's church.

In many places on the planet today, there are so many people coming to Christ that the Church must work together in order to get the harvest in before it is too late.

I know Pentecostals who will not serve with non-Pentecostals and non-Pentecostals who will not work with Pentecostals. I know Armenians who will not partner with Calvinists and Calvinists who will not network with Armenians. All along, they pray for harvest, believing the Lord will perform a miracle catch, but the nets are empty. I know others who say, "Our denomination/fellowship is growing each year!" Yet, their measurement is based upon where they were *then* and where they are *now*, instead of on how fast the world population is growing and how far we are falling behind the curve when it comes to finishing the Great Commission. There is not one single organization large enough to complete the Great Commission by itself. Thus, our measurement must be based upon the "we" instead of the "me."

I know this is a strong word, but it must be said today. The world population is exploding, and lost people are dying by the millions each year. What are we doing about it? We're forming committees and subcommittees to discuss evangelism methods and outreach programs! For twenty years I have heard leaders proclaim, "We must reach this generation for Christ!" Yet, year after year, the generation is *not* reached and most of our boats have little or no fish at all. What is it going to take for us to realize that we cannot bring in a God-sized harvest until we tie enough Christ-centered relationships together to handle the magnitude of the catch?

Did we finish the Great Commission when there were five billion people on the planet? No. Did we complete it when there were six billion? No. We did not come close. Will we repeat the same mistake now that the population is seven billion and growing? In our generation, the world population will increase to eight billion and then nine billion. What is the size of the net we are going to need to accomplish this global task?

The Christ-less leadership indictment today is that many are more willing to allow the harvest to be lost forever than to network together to bring it in. Most pastors and leaders don't mind working toward a Great Commission cause if the fish end up in their boat, meaning their own local church. But look at the story in Luke again. The other fishermen came and helped to calm the crisis—and they pulled in a huge harvest too! Simply stated, the whole harvest will never fit in one church or one organization alone. Our mighty Lord wants us to have a harvest of fish so large that local churches everywhere will have new converts in their worship services.

The bottom line for all of us is that we are called to finish the Great Commission. Think about what that means. There are over six million churches in the world today. That sounds like a big number. But if all those churches were somehow able to reach every living person for Christ, we wouldn't have enough room for all the new Christians to have a place to worship. We wouldn't have enough pastors to disciple them. The fact is, if we are even partly successful in fulfilling the Great Commission in any region of the planet in the near future, there simply are not enough churches and pastors equipped to help all the new converts to become Great Commission Christians. Yet, many Christian leaders will never cross the line to step into another pastor's world to synergize, network, and mobilize together because they are too afraid that some of the new fish will end up in the other pastor's boat.

Or worse, they're afraid that the *best* fish will end up in the other pastor's boat. "Lord, it's okay with me if You send some of the poor fish to other churches," they say, "as long as You let me keep the rich fish." Or, "Let me keep the big fish, and You can send the little fish over there."

The Christ-less leadership indictment today is that many are more willing to allow the harvest to be lost forever than to network together to bring it in.

How sad! If we are truly serious about fulfilling the Great Commission, then we're going to have to learn how to make the net work. We're going to have to learn how to put God's purposes first. We're going to have to learn how to synergize so that we might evangelize.

I remember so well when all of this became clear to me. In essence, you and I are *knot makers* in the Body of Christ. We are commissioned to tie relational knots worldwide to bring in the largest catch possible. If we're going to have a net, we must have knots. The more knots, the stronger the net. The stronger the net, the greater the catch.

During the summer of 2001, while making conference calls to invite pastors and Christian leaders to jump on board and get involved in the Billion Soul Network (www.Billion.tv), I spoke to the late Dr. Jerry Falwell, founder of Thomas Road Baptist Church and cofounder of Liberty University. His statement still rings in my spirit to this day. "We have been praying and fasting for a great harvest in North America but we're not prepared for that kind of harvest," he said. "If the Lord were to give us millions and millions of new converts in a given year, our local churches would not be prepared to bring in such a harvest, and therefore the harvest would be lost. Why would the Lord give us such a harvest if we're going to lose it? The reason I believe that we have not received the harvest is because we've not prepared ourselves for it."

That's the purpose of this book: to help us prepare for the amazing harvest that God has for the Church in this generation. It's a harvest much greater than any of us could ever take in on our own. It's greater than any one church, organization, or denomination could ever handle. To fulfill the Great Commission in our lifetime, we need more than our own boats; we need nets that work!

I encourage you to get prepared. Start tying knots. Begin building strong, relational networks that will allow you and your fellow leaders to synergize and minister in much greater capacity together than you could ever do by yourselves. Then cast your nets into the deeper waters and prepare to enjoy the victory together, as you witness *every* church—in your community and beyond—filling up with new Christ followers.

Establish Your Cause

In 2006, I made a trip to Lisbon, Portugal. While there, I arranged for a driver to take me to Palos, Spain. In order to get to Palos, you have to really want to go there; there is no direct route. It is a trip well worth the effort. In fact, I believe it's one of the greatest journeys a visionary leader could ever take.

For many years I had wanted to go to Palos, though I had never met anyone who had been there. Since I was in nearby Portugal, this seemed to be the perfect opportunity.

I got up early and left Lisbon at 5 a.m. so I could arrive at a specific monastery in Palos by 9 a.m. It was a beautiful summer day, and I enjoyed roaming around the ancient grounds looking at all the artifacts. After a while I walked into a small room that was about six by eight feet. Above the doorpost was a plaque with these words: "The Birthplace of America."

Like most people, I had always thought of Plymouth, Massachusetts, where the Pilgrims landed in the 1400s, as America's birthplace. Yet, this plaque said that America was actually born in this tiny room!

Stepping inside, it was as if I was trekking back more than five hundred years. The room was just as it had been in 1491. There were two chairs opposite one another with a table between them. Above the chair on the right was a portrait of Christopher Columbus. I looked closely at the painting for a few moments and then sat down in the same chair Columbus would have sat in back in 1491. I looked across the table at the chair where a Franciscan monk would have sat as he listened to Columbus sharing his vision of a New World.

Columbus believed he could find a new trade route to India across the Atlantic Ocean. If he was right, European ships would no longer have to make the long and torturous trip around the tip of Africa to get to the East Indies. Columbus was convinced this new trade route would be faster and safer.

The Franciscan monk caught Columbus' vision and took it to the King and Queen of Spain, who decided to fund it. Christopher Columbus got his boats and crew together, and the rest is history.

What is ironic is that Christopher Columbus was not Spanish. He was born in Italy and raised in Portugal. He had already taken the same vision to the Portuguese leaders, but they had laughed at him. They did not believe in the vision, much less the visionary. So Columbus went next door to Spain, where he found leaders who were willing to buy into the vision. As we all know, the vision of Christopher Columbus, funded by Spain, ultimately changed the course of human history.

I've often wondered, what if the Portuguese leaders had changed their minds? What if they had not laughed but had decided to fund the vision and the mission of Christopher Columbus? What would our world be like today? Would Americans be speaking Portuguese instead of English? We will never know.

When I left the monastery, my driver took me to a very old Catholic church that sat on the edge of a rock wall that, centuries ago, had backed up to the Atlantic Ocean. I knocked on the church door, and a lady who spoke no English answered. My Spanish driver became our interpreter.

"May I go inside?" I asked politely.

"Sorry, no guests today," she replied. "The priest is not here."

"Please, let me go inside," I asked again. "I have come a very long way."

"Sorry, the priest is not here," she repeated.

What she did not know is that sometimes I make coffee nervous! I can be quite tenacious.

"Please, call the priest and tell him that an American church leader has come a very long way. Tell him I would love to have just five minutes inside your church."

Finally, she agreed to call the priest. A few minutes later, she welcomed me in.

I believe in praying for big things in big places—places where men and women of old have taken bold steps for the glory of God.

Grateful for the opportunity to visit this ancient and beautiful church building, I immediately walked to the front of the sanctuary. I stood there in silence, realizing that I was standing at the very altar where Christopher Columbus had dedicated his men and his mission to God. This was the very spot where he had dedicated his cause to Jesus Christ! This was also the spot where, following his first expedition to the New World, Columbus returned to give praise and glory to God for all he'd been able to accomplish. I pondered the historic reality of this one man who, more than 500 years earlier, had been able to articulate a clear vision, establish and champion a cause, mobilize men and resources—and, in the process, change the world forever.

While I was on the premises of this historic site, I walked outside to a nearby grassy lawn and looked out over the Atlantic Ocean. This was where Columbus had assembled his men, boarded three simple boats, and left port. This is where he had begun his journey to cross the Atlantic for the very first time, opening the doors to a New World.

I knelt beside a fountain on the lawn and prayed. I asked God for big things. I asked Him to help us, His Church, to fulfill our vision. I asked Him to make our expeditions successful as we sought to complete the Great Commission. I asked Him to double the size of His Church so it would be harder for someone to live and die on this planet without hearing the glorious Gospel of Jesus Christ.

I believe in praying for big things in big places—places where men and women of old have taken bold steps for the glory of God.

A New Question

I often reflect on my trip to Palos, Spain, and this phenomenal story of Christopher Columbus. I share it with you now, in the beginning of this book on networking, because it illustrates the fact that a great mission needs a clear vision. Without a clear vision of a network's purpose, it won't work. It is important that we, like Columbus, articulate our vision and establish our cause. We need to understand why our network needs to exist. That's the beginning of our journey.

Columbus knew the "why" of his mission, and the result was "wow!"—the discovery of the New World. The fact is, until we answer the question "why," we will never get to the "wow!" No "why," no "wow!" The "why" question must be clearly answered if we expect to motivate men and women to commit to something that is greater than themselves. Too many Christian leaders spend their time asking, "What am I going to do and how am I going to do it?" and not enough time understanding, "Why should I do it in the first place?"

I would like to encourage you to take the time to read a familiar story in Genesis chapter 24. It is one of the greatest stories in the Bible for answering the "why" question and for understanding why we are to do what we do. In Genesis 24, Abraham was getting ready to graduate for eternity. He had only one thing on his mind before he died: he wanted to get a bride for his son, Isaac. He sent out his servant, Eliazar, on a mission to find Isaac a wife. Five times in the story, the Bible says that God gave Eliazar success. One translation says that God "prospered his path." I believe that God desires and has designed a prosperous path for you and for me. I believe he wants to prosper our networks.

It is important that our vision be clear and that we establish our cause, if our networks are going to have traction for the long run. The overarching reason for creating a network and for launching a networking ministry is to fulfill the Great Commission: to do what Abraham sent Eliazar to do and get the Bride and the Bridegroom together. That's a God-sized vision. It's the "why." If we have any other purpose, we are starting our network for the wrong reason. Anything less than reaching everyone on the planet with the Gospel and leading them to Christ is not a God-sized vision. We must answer the "why" before we can get to the "wow!"

I remember the first time the truth of this principle was driven home to me. It was the turn of the millennium, and my denomination was having its General Council in Indianapolis, Indiana. We had prepared long and hard, as we often did during the many years I served at our denominational headquarters. We started out with about 12,000 people at the General Council at the beginning of the week. By the time we got to the weekend, only 4,500 were still attending. That's not a good sign! You want your General Council to crest at the end—not on opening day.

Too many Christian leaders spend their time asking, "What am I going to do and how am I going to do it?" and not enough time understanding, "Why should I do it in the first place?"

After the General Council was over, we had a debriefing at our world headquarters. A committee of key leaders was gathered around a very long, distinguished boardroom table, and we were asked, "Why did the people leave? Why did the pastors not stay?"

When it was my turn to share, I was reluctant to say anything; but I knew that I had an obligation to speak up. This is what I said: "People do not come for the 'why.' They come for the 'wow.'"

"What do you mean?" a committee member asked.

"Well, the theme was 'wow,' but the speakers chosen were 'why.' In other words, the people didn't know why this speaker or that speaker—out of all the people available in the Body of Christ—was chosen to bring this particular message to this particular assembly." I went on to say that if we don't answer the question "why," then the people will not answer it for themselves. They'll just go away scratching their heads. "We must clearly answer why we're having the conference, why we're having the meetings, and why we're having these particular people speak on these subjects," I explained. "If the people understand 'why,' they'll come for the 'wow.'" Uncertainty will not motivate leaders to move forward. We must be clear, certain and causal in order to stir the will and emotions of great leaders.

Unfortunately, my answer was dismissed. It was not accepted as a possible answer. The accepted answer was, "It's a money issue. We're living in financially challenging times. The people couldn't afford to stay."

"People spend money on what they want to spend money on," I said. "But, they will not spend money on the question marks; they will spend money on the exclamation points."

It is clear to me after three decades that we must definitely answer the "why." We must establish our cause if we want others to come on board. So often we want to jump to the "how" before we answer the "why." We want to know how we're going to do it, how we're going to be successful, how we're going to build the network, how we're going to raise enough money to achieve the vision God has given us. But I believe that the bigger the "why," the greater the "how." I believe that when people understand "why," they will help us figure out "how." The "why" is the motivational factor. "Why" is what leads great men and women to do great things. If we fail here, we fail everywhere. "Why" moves us to the "wow!" It also leads us to the "how." Once we as Christian leaders understand why we're going to do something, God Himself will show us how to do it.

A New Network

On February 18, 2001, while I was driving home from the world headquarters of my denomination in Springfield, Missouri, I had what I consider to be one of my life's defining moments. The Holy Spirit quickened my heart to call the late Dr. Bill Bright, cofounder of Campus Crusade for Christ, to share with him the vision the Lord had placed in my heart for a global network of Christian leaders. I dialed the number and left a message with his assistant. Just over an hour later, Dr. Bright returned my call. We talked only briefly, discussing the global need for networking and for getting resources to pastors everywhere.

That was the first of many conversations. In those early days, we spent considerable time just trying to figure out the "big why" in order to release a "big how" for the global Church. From that day until now, I have never met a man more focused on why he was on the planet than Dr. Bright. Eleven months later, in January 2002, we cohosted the first-ever global pastors' conference with more than 5,000 pastors in attendance.

Think back to Eliazar in Genesis 24. Once Eliazar understood what the mission was and why he had to do it, he found out how to do it and God gave him great success.

When we were beginning the Billion Soul Network, it was crystal clear to us that we first had to establish our cause. We had to answer the big "why" if we wanted to attract others to become part of our network and make it *work*. We knew if we determined the "why," God would help us determine how to make the network prosper. So, we asked, "Why is this network needed? Why is it noteworthy? What is our cause?"

We invited other leaders to meet with us as we worked long and hard to flesh out our ideas. The result was that we established the cause. We answered the question, "Why?" Here is the "why" for the Billion Soul Network: We need to plant five million new churches and win a billion people to Jesus Christ to double the size of the Christian Church and finish the Great Commission in this century.

Why is the Billion Soul Network necessary? *To double the size of the Church and finish the Great Commission in this century.* How are we going to do that? *By planting at least 5 million new churches for a billion soul harvest.*

We answered the "why." We made it clear why we are here. We're not trying to copy somebody else and we're not trying to mimic another organization. We have a distinct reason for being. In the midst of answering "why," we began to discuss "how" we could turn "why" into "wow!"

We concluded that there are five "hows" to multiplying global value to the Body of Christ through our network. There are five ways that we can turn our "why" into "wow." This five-layer strategy was originally articulated by Dr. Paul Walker, former General Overseer of the Church of God, in Cleveland, Tennessee:

Layer 1: Relationships

Billion Soul provides relationship-building opportunities for the fulfillment of the Great Commission. We bring key leaders together to tie international knots for the biggest harvest in our lifetime. We seek out the best, most diverse relationships in the global Church and tie missional knots to expedite the growth of the global Church.

Layer 2: Resources

We promote shared resources for Kingdom-minded leaders worldwide. Billion Soul discovers and deploys the best resources, wherever they are found. In the past, world outreach has often been summed up as "the West going to the rest." At the Billion Soul Network, we believe in "the best around the world going to the rest around the world."

We believe in the global Church training the global Church. The best global teachers are not going to be found among a single small group. The entire Body of Christ must train the entire Body of Christ. We must all learn from one another.

Layer 3: Reports

We produce reports measuring the progress of the Billion Soul Network and sharing what's happening in the church around the world. Billion Soul co-chairs write and deliver reports about what is going on in their world region or area of ministry, and we get the word out to other leaders. We highlight what God's servants are doing in remote places and familiar places. We focus on various methods and models to show what works and what doesn't work. Dynamic testimonies of what the Lord is doing all over the world are made available on the web and through mail and email.

Layer 4: Recommendations

We prepare strategic recommendations for global partners, based upon experience and information. In other words, we say, "Based upon the knowledge we have, we recommend this tactic, this ministry, this organization, this method or model." We bring recommendations to the entire Body of Christ so that believers can learn from what others have already learned.

Layer 5: Research

At Billion Soul we publish current research for successful evangelism and church planting. Christian leaders are looking for reliable research that can help them make the best decisions for their churches and organizations. Our research is aimed to help them in their efforts.

In the past, world outreach has often been summed up as "the West going to the rest." At the Billion Soul Network, we believe in "the best around the world going to the rest around the world."

A New Strategy

The fact is that our strategy as a global Church must change. Let me explain why. For over 2,000 years the Church has worked to fulfill the Great Commission of our Lord. After all that collective labor, in A.D. 1900, just 49.65 percent of the world was evangelized. With another century behind us, more than 73 percent of the world has now heard the Gospel. Yet, there are still more than 2.4 billion people living today who have never heard of Christ.

Many church leaders are rushing to fill this great, unacceptable gap, and Billion Soul is working to do its part. Our cause, as we've stated, is to win a billion souls to Christ. Why should we race to win a billion more people to Christ in the next ten to fifteen years? Let me answer this "why" question for you through evangelistic growth and exponential growth.

Globally, if Christian leaders choose to continue with their present strategies, by A.D. 2200, 83 percent of the world will be evangelized. This appears to be great progress, until you realize that the world's population will exceed 9.5 billion people by the year 2050, and possibly reach 11 billion people by 2100. That means the unevangelized population will continue to increase over the next 100 years. The staggering fact is that at the current rate of growth, the global Church will win more than 3 billion people to Christ by 2100, and still more than 2 billion will be unreached, having never heard the Gospel even one time. When you compare Church growth to population growth, it becomes clear that the Church will not fulfill the Great Commission even by 2500 AD. Billions upon billions of people from near-future generations will die, lost forever.

If Christian organizations continue to try to win the world the way they always have—which has basically been to work separately, staying within their own denominations, groups, and spheres—then our children's children and their children's children will not come close to seeing our Lord's Commission finished in their lifetimes. This approach has brought us this far, but it will not take us to the finish line. What got us *here* will not get us *there*.

The fastest way to fulfill our Lord's command is to leave logos and egos behind and commit to working together.

In another scenario, though, the global Church could choose to synergize efforts and share resources. It could choose to *network*. And in fact, a growing number of Christian denominations and organizations— now numbering more than 1,450 and comprising more than 450,000 churches—have joined with Billion Soul in this effort. This network of pastors and leaders believes that it's possible to speed up Church growth by helping one another plant 5 million new churches and win 1 billion souls to Christ in the next ten to fifteen years. As a result, for the first time in modern history, many international Christian leaders are now saying it is realistically possible to complete the Great Commission in our lifetime!

As the global Body of Christ, we have the manpower. We have the resources. All we lack is the motivation. Thankfully, more and more leaders are becoming convinced that the fastest way to fulfill our Lord's command is to leave logos and egos behind and commit to working together.

This philosophy does not mean that we surrender our uniqueness in Christ or our doctrinal distinctiveness. It means that we retain our uniqueness, but we don't care who gets the credit—as long as God gets the glory! The goal is bigger than the role.

Our old traditional methods won't get us to the goal of establishing 5 million new churches within the next two decades. Traditional methods alone will not get us across the finish line. Only a networking strategy will move us from evangelistic growth to exponential growth, from traditional missions to global missions, and from showing our fellow laborers what we think they should do to serving our fellow laborers.

A New Measure

I believe that God is aligning his forces around the world for the greatest evangelism thrust in Church history. I see this everywhere I go, in every world region. By connecting resources and leaders across international, cultural, and language barriers, the Billion Soul Network is helping to create a new paradigm that demonstrates the evangelistic potential of synergy through relational ministry.

Many key global leaders have caught the Billion Soul vision. Dr. Jack Hayford, former president of The Foursquare Church and founder of The King's University in Van Nuys, California, wrote this some time ago in a letter to me: "I knew from our first meetings that this partnership would be more than just a cohort of like-minded leaders who hope to make some difference in the world. This has grown into one of the most embracing missional partnerships representing the diversity of the Body of Christ in Church history.

"We agree we must together find ways to understand and share the Good News with and to serve those for whom Jesus died and rose again. It blesses me when I see our brothers and our sisters as the Bride of Christ respond to the clarion call to be ready for the return of Jesus, through the fulfillment of the Great Commission."

Dr. David Sobrepena, founder of Word of Hope Christian Family Church based in Manila, the Philippines, is also Billion Soul's co-chair of Church Planting. He knows his topic; he has led church planting movements in his country by starting literally thousands of churches over the past eight years. What Dr. Sobrepena also knows is that church planting is already a strong and integral part of outreach in many countries outside the United States. The American Church has much to learn from the Church in the Philippines, Indonesia, India, and many other places in the world.

In fact, Dr. Stan Toler, General Overseer of the Church of the Nazarene in Kansas City, Missouri, made this observation: "Through our Billion Soul Network partnership, we're able to make available some of the finest resources in the Body of Christ today. The global tsunami wave of the future is not 'the West going to the rest' but 'the best going to the rest.' It is not about the West telling the rest of the global Church what to do or not to do; it is about synergizing for effectiveness, strategizing for evangelism, and sharing for equipping to finish the Great Commission. Today God's people around the world desire to work together more than they ever have done so before."

Statements such as these convince me that in the years ahead, the measurement of a ministry will not be found in the number of people worshiping in a pastor's local church, but rather in the number of dynamic partnerships he or she has built worldwide. God is raising up synergistic leaders to network throughout the earth!

What is going to happen in a region like Western Europe where Christianity has been in decline? Is there any hope that millions will come to Christ there or that thousands of churches will be planted? Will the United States cool down spiritually like Europe? Can America be turned around before it's too late?

Big questions deserve big answers. One thing we can rely on is that the global Church will never be any smaller than it was yesterday. Some missiologists today believe that the rise of global Christianity will impact not only Europe and North America, but the entire world. I believe this, and I've seen it. I'm convinced we're witnessing before our very eyes the rise of a global Church that is just as committed to fulfilling the Great Commission worldwide as it is to reaching individual countries or regions.

In the years ahead, the measurement of a ministry will not be found in the number of people worshiping in a pastor's local church, but rather in the number of dynamic partnerships he or she has built worldwide.

Do you realize that by 2030, 70 percent of global missions forces will not be from North America? In the single greatest missional shift in Church history, missionaries from every world region are heading to every world region. The last five years have seen the rise of some of the greatest church planting movements in the history of the world! Rest assured: the Great Commission will be fulfilled, and God will keep His promise. The day will come when the name of Jesus Christ is the most familiar name in all the earth.

This is why we work. And this is why we *net*work. This is why we serve; this is why we seek to add value to everyone else that we possibly can. I believe that in the future, those who are not networking will eventually be *not* working. Only the global Church can do what no one church, organization, or denomination has ever been able to do. Ours can be the generation that once and for all puts the cross of Jesus Christ on the roof of the world and lets the whole world know that Jesus Christ died for every person, every nation, and every people-group. When this is achieved, we will have a satisfaction that no previous generation has ever experienced!

We need to be motivated by what motivates Heaven. The church that has lost its purpose of winning the lost is lost itself. How many people will *your* network win? How many souls will your net catch? How many churches will you help to plant? How many missionaries will your church send?

We can achieve so much more together than we can ever do alone. Let's agree to synergize our efforts to finally bring the Bride to the Bridegroom. Can you think of anything more important to accomplish with your life? Can you think of any better reason for being? Can you think of any greater incentive to be motivated? The prophet Habakkuk exhorts us, "Record the vision and inscribe it on tablets that the one who reads it may run" (Hab. 2:2). May we do all that we can to establish our cause and make it clear, so that we can be used by the Lord to motivate great people to achieve greater things. Let's run with it together!

Examine Your Conditions

If I had a dollar for every naysayer who has said to me, "A global network cannot be built; it will not happen," I would be a wealthy man. At the Billion Soul Network we choose *not* to hang around with the critics and the cynics. We choose to hang around with those who believe that fulfilling the Great Commission can and *will* happen in our lifetime. We network with others and by doing so truly add net worth to them, to us, and to the global Church.

In Chapter 1 we identified the first step that we as leaders must take on the journey toward building an effective, synergistic network in the Body of Christ: establishing our cause. But once we have clarified our vision and answered the big "why," we can move on to the next step: examining our conditions. In Chapter 1 we talked about the "why." In this chapter, we're going to talk about the "where."

Think of Eliazar from Genesis 24. As he was preparing to fulfill the mission of his master Abraham, he understood the "why" question. His vision and his mission were clear. His challenge was to establish where he was—his current conditions—in order to determine how to get to where he needed to go.

How do we examine our conditions? How do we determine the zip code and the postal code of our life? How do we come to an understanding of where we are in time? I believe all great visionary leaders have a sense of where they are in time, and they are able to execute their vision in the window of time they have upon the planet. They have a sense of divine timing that leads to divine outcomes.

Knowing where you are is critical. What if you were to fly to Orlando, Florida, take a taxi to the middle of the city, then call me on my mobile phone and say, "James, I want to come and see you. Tell me, how do I get there?" The first question I'm going to ask you is, "Well, where are you now?" If you're not able to articulate where you are, then I'm not going to be able to give you directions to where I am. Now, if you call me and say, "I think I know where I am. I'm standing on the corner of *walk* and *don't walk*, I would reply, "Well, you've identified that you're on a street corner, but that is not good enough. I need to know your specific address in order to tell you how to get to where I am."

In order for us to move forward from establishing our cause, we need to examine our conditions. Where are we personally? Where are we professionally? Where are we spiritually, financially, relationally, geographically, and so forth? The better you can articulate the "where" of your life, the better you're going to be able to get to the "there" in your life. The "where" and the "there" is the distance between your two points of success. Once you understand "where," you can develop your plan to get "there."

In 1969, when the United States launched a rocket to send men to the moon, they didn't ask where the moon was at the time of the launch. They asked where the moon would be when the space capsule got there.

The better you can articulate the "where" of your life, the better you're going to be able to get to the "there" in your life.

Vision, like a rocket launching to the moon, has an arch to it. We cast the vision from the "where" of our current life situation to the "there," the place we're going to be. And of course when we get "there," we are now at the "where" once again. I've often said that if we cast a vision for the stars, we'll land on the moon. If we cast a vision for the trees, we will hit the ground.

I encourage you to take the time to ponder carefully where you are spiritually in your life. Are you a growing Christian? Notice I didn't ask if you were a growing Christian *leader*, but are you a growing Christian? Are you growing in the grace of the Lord?

Where are you financially? It's going to take a lot of money to establish and build a network that works. Not that you're not going to do fund-raising and friend-raising, but where are you financially today? Are you prepared to make the launch? Jesus said, "Count the cost first before you build the house." Cost is first. Construction is second.

Where are you geographically? I don't just mean where your address is or what zip code you are in. What is your world view? Where do you understand the world to be? Where do you believe the world is going?

Where are you relationally? Do you have a lot of friends? Do you know how to cultivate friends? Do you know how to invest value in people's lives? If you're going to be valuable, you have to learn to invest value. When people see you coming, do they see you as a deposit or a withdrawal?

A vision becomes a goal when you put a date to it.

Where are you positionally in the eyes of others? I'm not talking about the rank or position you hold in your company or your corporation or your organization. I'm talking about where you are positionally in the eyes of your friends and your neighbors. Do others see you as a believer and an achiever, a dreamer and a doer, or do they perceive you as someone who starts something but does not finish it?

When favor is high, labor is low. When favor is low, labor is high. It's not a matter of seeking a position or title. I have not carried a business card in my pocket for twenty years. I'm not concerned with passing out cards; I'm more concerned with how people view me as a person in their mind, in their heart, in their life.

So where are you? Once you understand where you are, I can tell you how to get to where I am. Once Eliazar understood where he was, he could then develop a roadmap that would get him to where he needed to go.

Set the G-O-A-L

A vision becomes a goal when you put a date to it. When I came to fully understand that some years ago, it changed the way I planned and organized my life, my ministry, and the network God had entrusted to Billion Soul. It's important that you have goals in your life. But are you able to think clearly enough to see far enough down the road of life to anticipate when your vision can be achieved? Can you see where "there" is?

At the Billion Soul Network we say that our vision is to help plant five million new churches for a billion soul harvest in the next fifteen years. We began September 18, 2005. We put a date on it. As a result, we're able to measure whether we're on time or not on time as we move forward.

A good way for us to examine our conditions and understand the "where" of our life is to use a simple acrostic: G-O-A-L.

G: Gather the facts.

Do the research. I've been accused of many things throughout my life, just as you have; but the one thing I've never been accused of is knowing too much. If somebody asks me a question, and I don't know the answer, I tell them I don't know. If I'm willing to tell them the truth when I *don't* know something, then they are more willing to believe me when I *do* know something.

It's important that we gather the facts. We need to understand our world to the best of our ability and be able to project where we see our world going. We need to understand the ministerial landscape of our lives and be able to navigate successfully. We need to understand who the key players are. Who are the "ministry mountains" that God has raised up around the world? If we're ever going to network with key "mountaintop" leaders, then we have to know who those leaders are in the first place.

We need to gather the facts technologically, gather the facts systematically, gather the facts financially, gather the facts relationally, and so on. We need to understand the facts of our network. We need to understand what it's going to take to make the network be what it can be, according to the vision and mission we have clearly articulated, so that people can fully understand and embrace it as part of their own life.

O: Organize a plan.

You cannot organize what you don't have, just as you can't teach what you don't know or lead others where you've never been. Some people like to set a goal and then believe that somehow, fatalistically, it will come together. But we need more than a goal; we need a plan, and we need to properly organize the plan. This involves three key elements: a *time* element, a *transition* element, and a *target* element.

Time. Life comes at us quickly. From time to time surprises come our way, both good surprises and terrible surprises. For this reason, when we organize our time, we need to put a buffer in: we need to add 20 to 30 percent of *extra* time to our schedule, just to plan for the unexpected. The alternative is to run out of time, which leads to people getting frustrated, aggravated and tempers flaring.

Always remember to add a little extra time when you make your schedule. Whatever you are planning to do in your network will probably take longer than you think. Life is lived forward and surprises come our way every day. Do the most important things first. Steven Covey, in his book, *The Seven Habits of Highly Effective People,* was masterful when he explained how we should put the big rocks of our life into our basket first; otherwise they will never fit, because of all the little rocks that always seem to appear out of nowhere.

Transitions. Because life is fluid, we need to have more than a good sense of time; we need to know how to make transitions. A masterful musician is triumphant in his transitions, flowing from one interlude to another, from one song to another, from one symphony to another. In a similar way, a master networker knows how to move from one task to another, from one event to another, and from one person to another. We have to learn that sense of transitional flow.

Targets. There are some people who like to shoot an arrow and then go draw a target around the point where the arrow landed.

Then they brag about their great aim. That's not planning! We need to establish clearly what our targets are ahead of time. If we don't determine what we want our outcomes to be, how will we know if we're successful or not?

For the Billion Soul Network, the target is all about planting churches. It's all about winning people to Jesus. Because we've identified the target from the beginning, we are able to articulate whether or not we're getting closer to it. We know whether or not there is fruit as a result of our labor.

When you organize a plan, make sure to consider all three elements: time, transitions, and targets. Then spend some time with the right people in the right place, and share clearly and succinctly what is on your mind and heart.

If we don't determine what we want our outcomes to be, how will we know if we're successful or not?

We all need three kinds of people in our lives. *Sounding boards* are people we can talk to and share our ideas with. They are the ones who will carefully and succinctly articulate what is good and what is not so good with our life and our plans. *Springboards* are people who will give us a hand up. They will help us pull things together, invite us to special meetings, and introduce us to key individuals. *Surfboards* are the ones who will ride life on the edge with us. They will move us forward and stretch us each and every day.

A: Act on the plan.

If you are like me, you can sometimes be timid or fearful when it comes to stepping out and acting on your plan. Early on in the networking process, I wondered, *If I step out, will I be successful? Will anyone want to participate in the Billion Soul Network?* There was a timidity, a fearfulness, that attached itself to my life. It took time for God to melt away the icy fingers of fear and for me to step out and believe that this mission, this network, could really add value in the Body of Christ.

We must overcome our fears, trust God, and act on the plan. Some networkers spend all their time trying to refine the plan and make the plan better. But as I stated earlier, life is fluid. The river of life never remains the same. It may not change its name; but when you step into it a second time, it's not the same river. Things have changed. So if you're waiting for everything to get just right, waiting for the advancement of technology, waiting for the advancement of world civilization, I can promise you that your plan will be out of date by then, and you will have to go back and redo it. Act on the plan, and act on it now!

Remember that we're *spiritual* networkers. That means that God puts providence in our plan. As we step out and move down the path He has set before us, He will bring great people and great resources along the way to help us. We can act on the plan with confidence. In fact, it is strategically important that we do so. It's important that we move forward each and every day.

L: Look back and review.

Earlier I said that we live life forward. That's true. We *do* live life forward, but we learn life backward. So after you've acted on the plan, pull your key people around you and take an honest assessment. Was it a good idea, or should you never bring it up again? What part is worthy of a repeat? What are some things you should not have done? Look back and review. Then, when you are done, set new goals.

Whenever you get "there," you have a new "where." As networkers, we are continuously walking through the process and planning of our life, the process and planning of our network. We establish the cause, we examine our conditions, and we continue to move forward. We learn more, and therefore we become better at what God has called us to do. We set new goals, always making sure that they are in sync with the God-sized goal of reaching everyone on this planet for Christ.

Take the Time

Giving serious thought to the "where" of your life and network will take time. It may take weeks or months; it may take a year. The key is to take whatever time is necessary to examine your condition and understand where you are, so that you can go where God wants you to go.

For me, that process began back in the mid-1990s. That is when I began to think about the ministry God had for me going forward; it's when I began to step out a bit from my personal "silo"—my own limited ministry sphere—to find out what else was available in the Body of Christ. And though it took me time to develop the ability to network with those outside of my denominational fellowship, I was determined to learn more about what I did not know. And out of that, the "where" of where I was became clear, so that I could understand where God wanted me to go.

In the last chapter, I told you about the day the Holy Spirit quickening me to make that first telephone call to Dr. Bill Bright of Campus Crusade. Notice, I had begun my personal examination in the 1990s; this call was made in February 2001. I was in a season of seriously assessing every aspect of my life. Should I be preaching and teaching or studying and traveling? During this period, I found myself becoming compass-driven instead of clock-driven. I was developing a sense of direction, not just a sense of activity.

I called Dr. Bright, and he and I agreed that we would serve together, work together, and form a network together. I remember getting home and telling my wife, Sheri, "The wind has changed direction. Our life will be different after today."

Eleven months later, we held our first conference in Orlando, Florida. Many naysayers had told us we were being premature. Others had advised us that the timing was bad, that pastors wouldn't fly to Florida. (It was just a few months after the terrorist attacks of 9/11.) But we were determined that we would not retreat. We believed that God was in this synergy—that God was in this network.

Five thousand pastors came to Orlando that January in 2002 from every state in the United States, every province in Canada, and many countries around the world, and a network was born. Dr. Bright and I were two men from two different walks of life and, frankly, two different generations. But we were determined to see the plan through to the launching of a network that would cast a big vision: planting five million new churches to bring a billion soul harvest and a doubling of the size of the global Church.

It took time for me as a Christian leader, as a Christian in general, to examine my condition and understand the "where" of my life. It also took time for us as a network to examine the network's conditions and have a sense of where we are, so that we are able to go where God wants us to go.

I encourage you to have quiet time with God and write down what the Holy Spirit prompts you to write, so that your networking mission might be formulated and crystalized in your heart, mind, and soul. Refine it and re-work it until you get it down to just a few simple sentences, because then you know that you really, truly understand it. Find those three friends—those sounding boards, springboards, and surfboards—and spend time with them too. Carefully examine your personal conditions and the conditions of your network. Gather, organize, act, and review.

Determine your "where" so that, with God's direction and help, you and your network will be able to get "there."

3

Embrace Your Commission

Small doors can open into big rooms. In 1994 I was asked to serve in a leadership position at the Assemblies of God World Headquarters in Springfield, Missouri. For twelve years I served as the denomination's Evangelist Representative, helping young and seasoned evangelists fulfill the Great Commission. It was a great journey and a wonderful opportunity for me to participate in such a visionary role. Over those twelve years I witnessed our Lord call more than 1,500 young evangelists into fulltime ministry.

These were not the only lives that were changed. As I look back to identify strategic moments and key junctures in my own life, I believe there came a defining moment for me as well, even though at the time I didn't fully realize it.

Less than one week after accepting this leadership role, I was asked to serve on a committee called the North American Conference for Itinerant Evangelists (NACIE). Dr. Billy Graham was the chairman of the committee and of the NACIE conference that took place about a year later. By accepting one role at our denominational headquarters, I was permitted to serve on this executive committee for about a year, relating to other NACIE leaders. It was on this committee that I began to make new relationships, many of which continue to this day and have become some of the closest of my life.

This is what I call moving from traditional missions to global missions. Regardless of who we are, each of us grows up in a personal silo, a personal context of what we know. It's not evil or negative; it's just a reality: we tend to be limited to our own sphere of the Body of Christ. But if we want to build networks that work within the global church, we must be willing to leave our silos and set out to learn about what we don't know and go where we have never been.

We must be willing to embrace our commission. When Abraham began to realize there was more in the world than Haran and more to know about God, he sought out this knowledge and truth. As he sought more, God revealed more to him. Even though the biblical context here is a personal relationship between a man and God, the principle rings true in the context of networking. As the Lord reveals a little to us and we seek Him for more, He will continually unfold more to us. I believe any pastor can develop a global networked church. Yet, it will take a certain emotional and mental fortitude to continue to seek God in order to bring the knowledge and truth of this into his or her world.

When Pastor Suliasi Kurulo, Billion Soul's Cochair for Oceania/Unreached Peoples, was a young man just beginning his ministry on the small Pacific island of Fiji, he was walking and talking to the Lord under a clear night sky. The Lord whispered to Suli, "Look at the stars above. Your ministry will become like the stars. Your work will be global, and the number of souls coming to Christ will be innumerable."

Suli planted his church in Suva, Fiji, in 1989, and named it World Harvest Centre. At the time of this writing, just over 20 years later, World Harvest Centre is one of the largest churches in the world. It has planted more than 3,000 churches in more than 100 nations. More than 200,000 members worship each Sunday through Harvest Centre and its daughter churches, many of which are located among formerly unreached people groups that Fijian ministers have evangelized. You see, Suliasi embraced his commission. He took ownership of the Great Commission and personalized it for his life and ministry. (His story is expanded in "The Global Networked Church" in the appendix of this book.)

Leaving Our Silos

In the early 1980s I moved from Mobile, Alabama, to Springfield, Missouri. For two and a half years I studied at the University of South Alabama before transferring to Central Bible College to complete my Bachelor's degree in Bible. This was my Abraham experience. I was stepping out to know and apply more. Later I also attended the Assemblies of God Theological Seminary to complete a Master's and Master's of Divinity before going to Trinity Evangelical Divinity School in Deerfield, Illinois.

When I moved to Springfield to attend Central Bible College, I was baptized into my denomination's view of global missions. I say this not to imply anything negative, but rather to articulate that while my own personal Christian worldview was enlarging, it was still in "the land of the familiar." If I had grown up in a different fellowship or denomination, whether large or small, I still would have been limited in terms of what I would have known of the Body of Christ. Thirty years elapsed before I obtained the broader Christian worldview that I have today.

From my perspective, most Christian leaders in this generation have a limited understanding of what comprises the global Church and where this massive army of Christ is moving today. Most do not understand that only about 5 percent of Christianity is in North America, while 95 percent is outside North America. The truth is, if all you know about is the 5 percent of Christianity that you have around you, then you do not know very much at all about Christianity!

If your denomination or fellowship happens to have a global thrust, then your knowledge of Christianity may be larger than another person's whose group has a smaller affiliation or perhaps no global association at all. For example, the Assemblies of God is the largest Pentecostal denomination today, with a membership approaching 70 million people across the globe. And yet, this number represents only 6 percent of the entire global Church. In this missional scope, a pastor who knows something about the 6 percent of the global Church, added to the 5 percent of the Church that is in North America, still has only an 11 percent understanding of the breadth and depth of the Body of Christ throughout the earth.

As my own Christian worldview was enlarging and I was beginning to understand and embrace my commission, small doors did open into big rooms. When I accepted the denominational responsibility of Evangelist Representative, I stepped through a door that revealed to me another Christian world that I was not familiar with at the time. When this world was revealed to me through my participation in the NACIE, I made the cognitive decision to learn more about it and to apply what I learned to my life and ministry. From that moment until today, I have yet to discover the end of the "big room."

Most Christian leaders in this generation have a limited understanding of what comprises the global Church and where this massive army of Christ is moving today.

We cannot embrace our commission and still stay in our personal silos. We must take that step into the big room. Let's look at it from another perspective. Let's say you're a fish growing up in a fishbowl. All you know are the other fish in the bowl. You are told, "*This* is the way you live your life. *This* is the way you go about your business." You are taught that the totality of the ocean of life is found within the parameters of the water in this fish bowl. Then one day a foreign fish jumps into your bowl and tells you that there is a vast, undiscovered world on the other side of the glass. You can choose not to believe him. You can choose to believe him and not care. Or you can choose to believe him and decide you're going to do something about it.

When you and I begin to learn about the rise of global Christianity, we can choose to believe it, not believe it, or try to discredit it through our doctrinal lens. Many leaders don't want to acknowledge that another world exists outside of their own fishbowl.

This mindset is one of the major reasons why the fulfillment of the Great Commission has not taken place in any generation.

Other leaders learn about the rise of the global Church and choose not to care. They are unmoved. In their minds, making the necessary changes that would be required over time to adjust their missional view and embrace their new commission would require too much emotional and mental effort.

If you decide that you are going to leap from your bowl into the ocean, please know this: all of your friends are not going to want to jump with you. They're not going to be as concerned about the ocean as you are. Is it still worth the leap? Absolutely!

I remember when I took that first leap and began to realize that there was so much I didn't know, so much about the Body of Christ I did not understand. There were so many Great Commission entrepreneurs that I had never met. As I set sail into this vast, unknown missional ocean, I began to bump into leaders of great vision and influence in the global Church, such as Suliasi Kurulo—leaders I refer to as "mountains of ministry."

Why "mountains"? In 2006 I was playing at one of Springfield's public parks with our five-year-old daughter, Olivia, whom we had adopted from China in 2002 at the age of 13.5 months. Six years later we adopted 27-month-old Priscilla, also from China. On this particular day, as any dad does with his little girl, I lifted Olivia up above my head to her great delight. While she giggled and laughed, smiling, I looked into her gorgeous Asian eyes. At that moment the Holy Spirit quickened me and said, "Look at what I've raised up all over the world."

A mental shift took place in my heart and life in that moment. In a matter of seconds, I was exposed to a panoramic view of what Christ had raised up. Not only has the Lord raised up phenomenal mountains of ministry around the world, but he has strategically raised them up in specific locations. If we don't know who these individuals are or where their ministries are located, then we will end up making the same tactical mistake that so many church leaders make: they go into various geographical regions intending to minister, but never connect with the people that God has already raised up in those places.

In the fall of 2010, a distinguished Christian leader and friend shared with me that he had just gotten back from ministering in Lagos, Nigeria. When he had arrived in Lagos, he had been greeted by his denominational friends. They'd all had a great time of fellowship and ministry, as thousands gathered together for a convention.

I know a number of key leaders in West Africa, so I named them and asked my friend if he had been able to meet with any of them. His response was that he'd never heard of any of them in his life! Understand, this man is a world traveler, a dear friend, and a great man of God; and yet, there he was, ministering in Lagos, Nigeria, and he had never met with—nor even heard of—some of the great Christian leaders God has already raised up there.

I share this not to be negative, but to force us to recognize that there is so much happening in the Body of Christ around the world that we simply do not know. We can spend years going in and out of a region and yet have no knowledge of what else the Lord is doing literally down the street!

Expanding Our View

How can we embrace our commission as leaders and networkers? I believe there are six steps.

1. Realization

Until you realize what it is you do not know, you cannot apply it or organize the particular aspects of it in your life.

Years ago, Dr. Bill Bright and I were sitting in his condominium having a conversation.

"James, I want to ask you a few questions," he said. "First, what do you consider to be the greatest privilege in your life?"

Quickly, I answered, "The greatest privilege in my life is knowing the Lord Jesus Christ."

"You've answered correctly," he said. "Here's the next question. What do you consider to be the *second* greatest privilege in your life?"

I didn't know the answer, and I tried to cover up by sounding spiritual. "I would like to go home and pray about this," I said.

Have you ever tried to cover up your ignorance? Have you ever tried to cover up what you did not know by cloaking it in spiritual terms? That's what I did that day—but Dr. Bright would have none of it.

"We don't need to pray about it," he said. "I know the answer to the question. The second greatest privilege in life is leading someone to the first greatest privilege in life."

It was so simple that it was profound!

Then he added, "I have one more question to ask you. Is your life a reflection of the two greatest privileges in life: knowing the Lord Jesus Christ, and leading people to the Lord Jesus Christ? If the greatest privilege is knowing Him and the second greatest privilege is leading people to Him, then our lives are to be a reflection of this."

The measure of our ministry's success is not the number of people in our churches. It's whether or not our ministry is really, truly moving the Church closer to fulfilling the Great Commission.

For years that conversation has spoken to me. It made me realize what I didn't know, and the focus of my life was changed in the process. Dr. Bright also said some words about himself that day that I will never forget. "If it did not help me to lead others to Jesus Christ, then I did not write it, I did not speak it, and I did not do it," he said. "If I had done otherwise, I would be wasting my life."

Dr. Bright was a Christian leader who understood what the great mission is—and what the Great Commission is. He was not an island unto himself. He realized that there's a great, vast world out there. He knew how very important it is that we understand God's world if we're going to fulfill God's will in His world.

We must come to the realization that the measure of our ministry's success is not the number of people in our churches. It's certainly not what people say about us. It's whether or not our ministry is really, truly moving the Church closer to fulfilling the Great Commission. If what we are doing is not moving us closer to reaching the whole world for Christ, why would we want to do it anyway?

Do you realize what you don't know? Here are some questions you can use as a gauge. Do you understand what the Great Commission is? Do you have an understanding of the current prevailing worldview? Do you know how many denominations and Christian organizations there are in the world? Do you know what the number one mission-sending nation is? Do you realize what is going to be required of you in order to form relationships in persecuted regions of the world, versus more friendly and stable regions? The fact is, in order to say you have a net that works, it has to work not just in the easy places but in the hard places; not just where people have heard, but where people have never heard.

Until we embrace our commission and realize what it is
we are called to do, we will never obtain the focus,
the fortitude, the faith, and the finances we will
need to achieve it.

Do you know the difference between an un*saved* person and an un*reached* person? Do you know where the unreached people groups are on the planet? Do you know what it means to adopt an unreached people group? Do you comprehend what it's going to take to network among the unreached, versus networking among the reached?

For many, this idea of people groups is new, so let's expand our knowledge a little further in this area. Do you know that this world that God loves is made up of approximately 16,000 different people groups? Most of us tend to think of populations in terms of countries or nations or regions. But during the Second International Congress on World Evangelization in 1989 (often referred to as Lausanne 2), over 4,000 key Christian leaders met in Manila to discuss how the Church around the world could fulfill the Great Commission. The result was a determination to move from a view of evangelizing *nations* to a view of reaching *ethnos*—people groups. This approach is actually more in sync with the New Testament than the approach of carving out areas of geography and saying, "Let's work in different regions of the world."

Out of these 16,000 or so people groups that exist in the world, about 6,000 are considered to be "unreached." By definition, an "unreached people group" is one in which less than one-tenth of one percent of its population has been provided an adequate witness of the Gospel of Jesus Christ. Does it bother you to know that about half of the world's people groups are unreached?

Here's another way to look at it. There are approximately 2.4 billion people in the world who have yet to hear the name of Jesus Christ for the first time. They may have heard of Microsoft, Coca-Cola or Mickey Mouse, but they haven't heard the name of Jesus. Does that challenge you in your networking? It should. If we are about the Lord's work of creating a net of relationships for the purpose of harvesting, then we have to understand where the harvesting is most needed. Otherwise, how will we ever fulfill the Great Commission?

Let us continue to expand our global view. Out of those 6,000 unreached people groups in the world, over 600 of them comprise the largest unreached people groups in the world. They range from groups with as few as 100,000 people to some with populations in the millions. And of the 600 largest unreached people groups in the world, 310 of those are in Northern India between Pakistan and Nepal. I'm highlighting this because we need to realize what we don't know! If I could create only one missional bull's eye to target my arrows, I would have to say that Northern India is the darkest place in the world today; we must have its people groups in our sight.

What does all of this information have to do with developing a network that works? It has everything to do with it, if we believe that we're called to work with our fellow leaders in the

Body of Christ to help fulfill the Great Commission. Until we embrace our commission and realize what it is we are called to do, we will never obtain the focus, the fortitude, the faith, and the finances we will need to achieve it.

2. Realignment

Once we reach a level of realization, we need to have a realignment of our lives to point toward what really matters to our risen Lord. None of us can do everything, and none of us can be everywhere. So we have to decide, how we are going to use our time, our talent, our treasure? What are we going to be about?

The most challenging aspect of realignment has to do with relationships. I call it the "Great Relationship Exchange." Remember the fish in the bowl? Many times, leaders—and especially networkers who have chosen to grow and mature in their global understanding of the Body of Christ—find that others do not want to go with them on the same journey.

Once we realize the weight of the Great Commission and choose to embrace it, sooner or later we will have to reach out and connect with others who are like-minded in order to achieve the objective.

One of the most painful aspects of my networking journey has been the realization that not everybody is Great Commission-minded or Great Commission-motivated. There came a time in this process when I had to make some relationship exchanges. I still consider those who did not take the leap with me to be friends and faithful followers of Christ, and I believe they consider me their friend as well. But, they're not my intimate friends, my Great Commission friends. They're not my networking fellow-laborers. They're not my co-laborers amongst the unreached peoples.

This realignment in my relationships took time to figure out. I had to decide who I was going to invest my life into, and who I was going to allow to invest their life into me. I had to be willing to let go of some from my previous inner circle of friends and exchange them for those God was bringing my way. This has been one of the hardest exercises I've ever gone through—and I expect I will go through it several more times before I graduate for eternity.

Am I inferring that if someone chooses not to network, that they are out of step with the Lord in their Christian life? Not at all. What I *am* saying is that once we realize the weight of the Great Commission and choose to embrace it, sooner or later we will have to reach out and connect with others who are like-minded in order to achieve the objective. The size of our expanded circle will be determined by our specific role in God's goal.

As I write these words, I am going through a painful relationship exchange. I have watched a fellow leader build a business, write books, and make claims that he is concerned with God's world. Yet it has been two years since I asked him about having his writing translated and placed into the hands of those who need it the most. He has not taken a step in that direction. I also watched firsthand as he invited key leaders to come and speak for his organization, but he only ministered on the surface level to them; he did not invest deeply into them. Sadly, I have come to the conclusion that this man will make it to heaven, but he will do little to help others get there.

As we choose to realign our lives to what matters most in this life and the life to come, we become more focused on the eternal and less focused on the temporary. So get ready; some will choose not to include you in their circles, because you will make them uncomfortable about their own lack of focus and follow-through on winning souls—and their unwillingness to not care about who gets the credit.

3. Reproduction

The third step in embracing our commission is reproduction. I remember praying during the last week of 2009, "Lord, make me productive next year." I sensed the Lord whisper to me, "Do not ask Me to make you productive. Ask Me to make you *re*productive. Do not produce anything that's not worthy of reproduction." Coming out of that simple quiet time, I determined to spend the rest of my life not producing but *re*producing. I would no longer produce anything that was not worthy of reproduction. That simple word from God has brought greater focus and greater faith to my life.

Reproduction needs to be a goal not only in our lives, but in our networks. New systems sometimes become complicated and cluttered—making them impossible to reproduce in other places with other people. We need to have networks that are flexible and limber. The systems we develop must be lean and mean, rather than weighty and bulky. All the great systems of the world are simple. By simple, I don't mean shallow. The great systems of the Body of Christ, where the Church is reproducing and the Great Commission is flourishing, are uncomplicated environments where creativity has a chance to blossom, and people are able to participate on multiple levels.

Success isn't measured by how much we produce; it's measured by how much we reproduce.

Once we have developed a system that is sustainable, we will have the time we need to ponder and process the best possible methods for making our net work in the world. It seems that most leaders are running so fast, they have little time to think, "Is there a more efficient method for achieving a reasonable amount of success?" Remember, success isn't measured by how much we produce; it's measured by how much we *re*produce. It's measured by how far we are able to advance the Great Commission in this generation.

4. Repetition

Once we have developed systems that reproduce themselves, we can then truly begin repetition. As a network, one of the key aspects of Billion Soul is its ability to mobilize fellow leaders. The more people we can equip to repeat the same or similar things in the advancement of greater outcomes, the more catalytic we become everywhere we go. If you are committed to building a network in your city, then you must mobilize in your city. If you desire to build a regional network, then you must mobilize within that region. If you're building a network for the world, then you've got to be able to mobilize key people and their followers throughout the world.

In recent years much has been written on leadership and the influence of it. Yet, leadership is not just influence but the ability to mobilize people for a cause greater than themselves. Just because a person writes a book about a subject does not mean that he or she has motivated anyone to act on what they have read. Leaders don't merely influence; they mobilize.

Small dreams never enflame the hearts of great people. I hope that becomes one of your key mottos, one that you hang on your refrigerator door or put in a prominent place in your office. Small dreams never enflame the hearts of great people. For you see, we attract what we are, not who we want. If we attract the most negative people on the planet, it's because we've become negative ourselves. If we attract small people, it's because we're projecting small dreams. If we don't like who we're attracting, then we must change what we are.

In order to be effective knot-makers, then we have to be able to attract the kind of people that we want to tie together. This key networking skill must be mastered if we plan to achieve any level of significance and success.

5. Reevaluation

On the heels of repetition, there should be reevaluation. As I've said previously, life is lived forward and learned backward. We must reevaluate, "How much did it cost in time and treasure to achieve this particular outcome? How much energy was required to move the effort forward to this degree?" Jesus said, "We must count the cost before we build the house. Wise is the person who understands what it does cost." There needs to be evaluation as we begin each effort, and reevaluation after we achieve each goal.

6. Renewal

The last step in embracing our commission is renewal. When we and our networking team achieve victory, we should celebrate—and renew our commitment to keep going to the finish line. I've learned that people realize what we consider to be important by what we choose to celebrate. Whether it's in our office with our staff, in a public meeting with our friends, or at our organizational headquarters with our colleagues, celebration helps the people around us understand what we're committed to. It also demonstrates to people everywhere what we believe are the most important aspects of the Christian life.

Some years ago, before the passing of Dr. Jerry Falwell, I spoke at the Convocation at Liberty University, which I consider to be one of the greatest Christian universities in the world. More than 10,000 students, professors, and leaders were there. Following my presentation, a young man walked up to me and handed me a note on a piece of paper. "If you don't mind, please read it on the way to the airport," he said.

As I headed to the airport, I took out that piece of paper and began to read. What the young man wrote turned out to be some of the most profound words on success I've ever read. This is the essence of his note: "Dr. Davis, thank you for taking your time and coming and investing your energy and creativity into our student body today. I've come to understand that failure is succeeding in the wrong things. But success is succeeding in the right things. We're all going to be successful; but are we going to be successful in the right things, or successful in the wrong things?" Those simple words changed my perspective on what I've come to understand as true success and true failure.

It is possible for us to build a great network that is not a Great Commission network. It is possible to build a network that is not focused on evangelism and disciple-making. It is possible to build a network yet never take the Gospel to the four corners of the earth. When we choose to embrace our commission, we must choose to be about the mandate of the Master. That is the only true measure of success.

4

Enforce Your Character

Moral earthquakes are the result of secret faults in a person's life. When unforeseen pressure is applied and a spiritual collapse occurs, great is the loss to that person's family and ministry for years to come. When you and I choose the networking path, we must recognize that much is at stake each day of our lives. If we are not careful, we can pick up the sordid dust from dirty trails. Instead we must make every effort to discipline our lives and enforce our character. We must make sure that we have proper spiritual cleansing, so that we can "grow and go" instead of "dry and die." We do this in three ways.

1. We must discipline our personal decisions.

Eleazar, Abraham's servant, did this in Genesis 24, as he set forth to accomplish a seemingly impossible mission for his master. He disciplined his life and his personal decisions. When he saw Rebecca, he did not rush to judgment; he sought God and carefully considered whether she was the right wife for Isaac. When we are making personal and professional decisions, we must be wise and do our due diligence before coming to a conclusion.

2. We must discipline our personal desires.

There are times when we must set aside ballgames, television, vacations, and so on, to do what is necessary to accomplish our task. Eleazar fasted and prayed throughout his mission. We must make prayer and fasting a priority too. We do not stop to pray; we simply do not stop praying. There is no easy or fast way to achieve what God has put before us. We must pray our way to success and prosperity in our life and ministry.

3. We must discipline our personal directions.

Once Rebekah was chosen, Eleazar prepared to finish his mission by returning with her to Abraham. Rebekah's family tried to talk him into waiting a few days but Eleazar responded, "Do not delay me, since the Lord has prospered my way. Send me away that I may go to my master" (Gen. 24:56). Eleazar disciplined his personal direction by disciplining his time.

Do you think God would tell us to do something and not give us enough time? Do not squander your time, personally or professionally. If your professional life outpaces your personal life, then you will have stress, and you will bring stress to other people. We must always continue to grow and go. We must not pull over and park in life.

Eleazar also disciplined his personal direction by making the best use of his skills and gifts. Abraham did not send his servant off on the mission without giving him the gifts that were necessary to get the job done. Do you think God would call us to bring a bride to Jesus Christ and not give us the skills and gifts we need to be successful? God has given us gifts, not toys. We are to use these gifts to help fulfill the Great Commission. There are too many people who are wasting their gifts and getting little in return!

The Rules of the Networking Road

As we set out on the networking journey to connect the bride and the bridegroom, we need to know the rules of the road so we can successfully get to where we need to go and complete our mission. When I think of character counting in every aspect of our lives, I often reflect on the life of Joseph. In a later chapter we will focus on the end of Joseph's life, when he gathered his family around him and made them promise to take him with them when they left Egypt. There was also a time earlier in his journey when he was falsely accused and suffered many years for it. Eventually, he was exalted to second in command of one of the greatest empires of all time. Throughout his life, Joseph often found himself in uncharted territory.

We have all found ourselves in uncharted territory at one time or another. I'm sure you've had the experience of driving in a new city, coming to an intersection, and not knowing which direction to go. As I have traveled across this country and around the world, I have found that some things about driving are the same everywhere.

The lights sometimes don't seem to work right. You can count on that. You'll be driving in the late hours of night, when no other cars are around, and you will sit at a long light while it runs its full cycle.

The signs don't seem to be written for visitors. It is obvious they were written for the local folks. You will think that some signs are out of place and others are missing altogether.

Local people have a hard time giving directions. I once asked a man how to get around a detour on a street that I knew how to travel. His instructions were, "Take this other street, make a right, then follow your nose to the church."

As networkers, we are constantly traveling an uncharted path, since we are striving to connect various leaders to accomplish assignments together that they could never do alone. We are constantly coming up to new intersections and having to make decisions on which way to go. Many leaders come to the corner of temptation and desire and make the wrong turn. Then they spend many years of life on dead end side streets rather than on the right track. You may have faced that intersection today or yesterday or the last tax filing day. Did you make the right turn and exemplify godly character or did you make the wrong turn?

Joseph was raised to be obedient to the teaching of God that had been placed in his heart. Wheeling through life, everything seemed to be going great for him. He was enjoying the beautiful scenery, the breeze in his hair, and the drive through the beautiful mountains. Suddenly, the mountain top turned into a deep, dark valley as his brothers sold him into slavery, relocating him a thousand miles from home in the pagan world of the Egyptians.

His next great encounter with the intersection of temptation and desire occurred in Potiphar's house. It was there that Joseph demonstrated for us how to enforce our character and how to live the kind of life that is pleasing to God. I want to share with you five rules that will keep you on the righteous road. These are the same rules that you and I need to practice along the networking path to global success.

As networkers, we are constantly traveling an uncharted path, since we are striving to connect various leaders to accomplish assignments together that they could never do alone.

Rule #1: Read the Map

It's important that we know the rules of the road, that we read the map, and that we know the directions before starting the trip. God had put a dream in Joseph's heart and showed him his future. He knew where he was going and he decided to be faithful to God's plan for his life. He didn't wring his hands and try to figure out what to do when he faced the intersection of temptation and desire. He knew what he would do before he ever got there. He had already read the map and knew the directions. What dream has the Lord placed in your heart?

There are those who are on the righteous road to heaven and those who are on the road to ruin and hell. Some have chosen to make the right decisions that will ultimately take them to heaven to be with Christ. Others will continue to make wrong choices that will take them to the eternal place of suffering called hell. If we want to be on the road to heaven and avoid the road to hell, we've got to read the map.

We've got to know where we're going and put first things first in our lives. Joseph knew the map and he knew he had to stay on course. There are a lot of people who live wasted lives and wish they could do it all over again. Unfortunately, most of them would do just that: waste their lives all over again! Someone once said that the greatest privilege is life and the second is having the privilege of directing that life. God gives us that privilege; that's why it's important to know the directions beforehand. There will be times in leadership when people will try to lead us down the wrong path. There will be times when they will try to get us to exchange our God-given roles and goals for their dreams and drives. People will change but God's Word never changes.

Rule #2: Stop at the Red Lights

Do you know what happens when people run red lights? Someone gets hurt. Joseph came to the red light of fornication and adultery and said "no" to heartache and disappointment. Did you know that the hardest word in the English language to pronounce is not "antidisestablishmentarianism"? The hardest word is "no." We live in a culture that does not resist sin and believes having the Ten Commandments hanging on the school walls will take the fun out of life. The Ten Commandments are not ten suggestions. God is trying to stop us from hurting ourselves.

Wrapped up in the Ten Commandments are various kinds of relationships. The greatest pain that people can suffer does not involve their jobs, their education, their finances, where they live, or the cars they drive. I believe the greatest pain that people can suffer is the pain of broken relationships. If we are going to have the kinds of relationships with God and with one another that He intends, we must learn to stop at the red lights. When we run the red lights, we hurt ourselves and others and we sin against God.

Running the red lights of life results in fractured homes, broken dreams, and shattered hearts. Approaching the intersections of life with blatant disregard and a know-it-all attitude only leads to sorrow. If you think that you can ignore the stop signs and no accident will ever happen to you, you are setting yourself up for conflict and much pain. In time, the accident will surely happen and it will ruin lives, families, and the plans that God has for your life. God places red lights in our path to save us from tragedies. Joseph came to his red light and said, "Stop." He was willing to do what God wanted him to do.

As networking leaders, we have to build a godly circumference in our lives. The expectations upon us are high. If we don't have a biblical bedrock as our foundation, eventually our spiritual house will collapse under the pressure and strain of developing a network that works. Running red lights will eventually bring death and destruction.

If we don't have a biblical bedrock as our foundation, eventually our spiritual house will collapse under the pressure and strain of developing a network that works.

Rule #3: Yield the Right of Way to Others

There are times when neither you nor I will be first in line, when we will have to yield to others. Joseph yielded the right of way. He respected Potiphar and the relationship he had with him. He didn't want to do anything that would violate that relationship.

Not only that; he yielded the right of way to Potiphar's wife and chose not to violate her. He also respected himself and did not want to commit sin against God. He said, "There is no one greater in this house than I" (Gen. 39:9). He understood that God had put him there and had a plan for his life. Do you know what happens when someone commits sexual sin? They lose self-respect. That's the first thing that goes. They don't have the same respect for themselves they once had and every aspect of their lives is impacted. Joseph understood the importance of that respect.

When we fail to yield the right of way to others, when we fail to live with a servant's heart in all that we do, people get hurt, including ourselves. And when we fail to yield the ultimate right of way to God, the suffering is much worse.

I remember the day my wife and I saw the heartbeat of our unborn daughter on the hospital monitor. I thought about how many times that little heart would continue to beat—on the day she would come into this world, the day she would first go to school, the day she would graduate from college. That heart would perhaps beat a little faster the day she found the love of her life, the day she married, and the day she had a child of her own. But one day that heart might become sick and miss a beat; one day it might need a pacemaker. And one day that heart would beat no more. Maybe it would stop beating when she was driving on Main Street, or lying in a hospital, or sleeping peacefully in her bed one night.

Eventually, every one of us will kiss the face of death. We are all only one heartbeat away from eternity—from heaven or hell. And yet so many people live their lives as though they will never die. They refuse to yield their lives to God. The great missionary C.T. Studd once wrote, "Only one life, 'twill soon be past, Only what's done for Christ will last." Make up your mind that you are going to live your life for the only One who can give you a fulfilling life now and a redeemed life for all eternity.

Rule #4: Submit to the Proper Authority

There is a biblical principle I often repeat: You cannot be over the things God wants you to be over until you are under the things God wants you to be under. What are the things God wants you to be over?

God wants you to be over the works of the flesh. The way to get over the works of the flesh is to be under the rule of the Lord Jesus Christ. When you and I get under Jesus, then we get over the works of the flesh. For the Christian, under means over.

God wants you to be over the power of the devil. You cannot be over the power of the devil until you're under the authority of the Lord Jesus Christ. Joseph teaches us this lesson. "How then could I do this great evil and sin against God?" he said (Gen. 39:9). Because he was submitted to God, when he came to the corner of temptation and desire, God helped him to navigate the intersection successfully.

Ultimately, in the private times of life, it's our love for God that keeps us pure. We must cultivate a love and passion for God. We must discipline ourselves and practice being submissive to God.

Then, when temptations come, as they surely will, we will be over-comers. Too many of us think that we have rights but no respon-sibilities. We want to do whatever we want to do and not be re-sponsible for our sins. We are quick to blame our failures on the way we were brought up, our race, our economic status, or our environment. Remember, Adam and Eve lived in a perfect world, yet they chose to rebel and sin against God. The problem isn't our environment; it's our lack of surrender to Jesus Christ.

Some of us only want Jesus to be our Savior, but He wants to be the Lord, Captain, and Commander of our lives as well. He knows how to protect our lives and keep us pure every day. When we get under Jesus, we get over Satan. Joseph proved victorious in the face of temptation, even though it meant some personal disappointment, heartache, and more time in the dun-geon. Because he remained faithful and pure, God blessed and fulfilled His plan for Joseph's life. What would have happened to Egypt and later to Israel if Joseph had sinned against God? God wants our Christian lives to have a positive impact on oth-ers, not a negative impact. When we learn the power of being under, we will have greater power for being over. We are called to serve our fellow servants.

Rule #5: Look Both Ways and Then Go

It's not a good idea to pull into the middle of an intersection and then start asking for directions. As soon as Joseph came to the intersection of temptation and desire, he ran as fast as he could. He left his coat, but he kept his character. He left his vest, but he kept his virginity. You can only lose that once. Some of us think we are tough enough to hang around and handle temp-tation when, in fact, we should flee. The Apostle Paul said to flee immorality, to run from it.

Are you in the middle of an intersection right now and trying to decide which way to go? If the direction is displeasing to God, run from it and be true to the Lord. Keep your heart pure and your character intact. God is looking for leaders who are will-ing to enforce their character in a world that has gone wild. Life is a series of intersections and God wants you to make the right decision and stay pure at every one.

In fact, Jesus, the greatest Leader of all time, has demonstrated for us how to navigate the tests and trials of life.

He read the map and knew the directions. Everything He said and did was at the bidding of His Father; He never spoke or acted of His own volition. He knew the words and plans of God for every action and activity of His life, death, burial, and resurrection.

He stopped at red lights. He never sinned once. He obeyed all the principles found in the Word of God. He was spotless. He was sinless. He knew what it meant and what it took to stop at the red lights.

He yielded the right of way to others. He was a servant. When He washed the disciples' feet, He showed them that it was not time to rise to the throne, but to reach for a towel. He knew what it was to yield the right of way to others.

He submitted to the proper Authority. Jesus said, "I only do what My Father tells Me to do; I only say what My Father tells Me to say. I am under authority. Just as you are to be under authority, I am under authority. I submit Myself to proper authority every day." He responded properly at every juncture.

He looked both ways and went ahead. Calvary was the greatest moral intersection of all time. It was there that the light turned green and "whosoever will" could have eternal life. Jesus knew what had to be done to accomplish our salvation. He looked both ways and went ahead to the cross to make our redemption possible.

The Road of No Regrets

William Borden was born in 1887, the son of the founders of the Borden milk company, which is still around today. His family attended the famous Moody Church in downtown Chicago when R.A. Torey was the pastor. William grew up in a very wealthy, influential home. When he graduated from high school, his parents sent him on a world cruise so he could experience the other cultures of the world. For months he wrote letters to his parents describing what he was seeing and learning. In time, however, the tone of his letters began to change. He began to write about the lost people of the world. He wrote about the poor, the less fortunate, and those living in poverty. Upon his return home, he announced that he felt God was calling him to preach the Gospel as a missionary to Mongolia. He said that he did not know if he would be successful, but he wanted to do his best for the Lord Jesus Christ.

The Bordens had planned for William to someday take his father's place as head of the milk company. Nevertheless, they supported his call to preach. While studying for the ministry at Yale, he gave away his fortune so others could afford to attend college. Then he wrote inside the cover of his Bible two words: "No reserve."

After four years at Yale and four more years in seminary, his family begged him to stay home and take over the milk business for his ailing father. He responded that he could not turn back; he had to do his best for Jesus, who had done His best for him. Just before leaving by ship for Egypt, he wrote two more words inside his Bible: "No retreat."

Ultimately, life is not lived in length—it's lived in the depth of our relationship to the Lord Jesus Christ.

While in Cairo visiting friends, he contracted a fatal disease and died within one month. He never got to preach as a missionary. Instead, his body was shipped home for a funeral led by R.A. Torey. After the funeral, the pastor gave William's Bible to his parents, who now saw three sets of words written inside. "No reserve" was written when William was at Yale. "No retreat" was written when he left home to go to the field of his calling. And "No regrets" was dated just before he died.

Many ministers live with regrets about their marriages, their families, their children, their careers. I want you to know that when you do your best to live for Jesus and serve Him with a heart of true devotion, purity, and obedience, at the end of life's journey you will be able to say, "No regrets, because I did my best for Jesus." Ultimately, life is not lived in length—it's lived in the depth of our relationship to the Lord Jesus Christ. As master networkers, we need to enforce our character so that our lives and our ministries bring honor and glory to Christ alone. That's how we will fulfill the Great Commission in our lifetime. That's how we will build a net that works.

5

Engage Your Creativity

Jesus came down from the star-spangled skies of glory. He was born in Bethlehem, hidden in Egypt, raised in Nazareth, baptized in the Jordan, and tempted in the wilderness. Christ performed miracles on the roadside, healed multitudes without medicine, and charged nothing for His services. He conquered everything that came up against Him. Then Jesus Christ took our sins up to Calvary and died on the Cross for the world. He was buried in Joseph's new tomb and on schedule rose out of the grave with the power of His omnipotence.

These highly creative images from the Bible were chosen by God in order to communicate with us. Not only are the words inspired, but I believe the pictures and images the words create in our minds are also inspired.

If we are going to build a net that works, we need to know how people learn. Generally, people perceive with the right half of their brain and process information with the left half of their brain. Word pictures connect both halves. As the 1930s philosopher William MacNeile Dixon once said, "The human mind is not as philosophers would have you think, a debating hall, but a picture gallery." God created us to understand truths from pictures painted in our minds. The mind believes more in images that are seen than in words that are heard. That's why Bible stories from Genesis to Revelation are filled with pictures of a loving God who communicates to His world. When Jesus was born in Bethlehem, His birth was an outward expression of the inward thoughts of God. Jesus is the picture of the essence of who the Father is. "If you see Me," Jesus said, "you have seen the Father."

Our God is a creative God, and He calls us to be creative as well. Our challenge as leaders and networkers is to find creative ways to bridge the past to the present, so that all people can understand, comprehend, and apply biblical truth to their lives.

Today's preachers must serve as the filter from the text to the times, from the ancient past to the technological present. If the images we present do not have a biblical basis, of course, then they do not have the authority of God behind them. We must be biblical, yet practical. We must recognize that the development and deployment of computers and the Internet have shaped the way people think more than yesterday's presenters could have ever imagined. In order to biblically network, we must talk the language of today's average listener in this image-rich Google world, recognizing that a Bible passage will generally have only one meaning, yet many applications. The meaning is biblical and does not change. The application of it, and the presentation of it, however, must change with the times.

Creativity in Presenting the Message

Some networkers, for the lack of knowing what to say, choose to rely on technological gadgets and film clips to make up for their lack of preparation and thought. They put all kinds of bells and whistles in their messages, yet there is no depth in their theme. There is no meat in their message. It is like a fire truck going by with no firemen on it; there is a lot of noise, but no one is saved. Shallow gimmicks are no substitute for being truly creative.

Then there are those networkers who continue to focus primarily on what to say but have not changed their style in the last twenty-five years. They've done nothing to update how they package what they're saying. Neither group is engaging their creativity.

Our God chose to communicate to humanity through Christ, who was born like every other human. He chose this path to build a bridge between His world and our world, so we could know Him and have eternal life. God knew what He was going to say, and He took great pains to *say* it and *show* it in a way that we humans could understand. You and I must follow His example.

Over the centuries there have been highly sophisticated hermeneutical debates on the summary image of the Old Testament and the New Testament. Many scholars believe the Old Testament points us forward to Jesus Christ and the New Testament points us back to Jesus Christ. Other Bible scholars stress that the Old Testament revealed God the Father, the New Testament revealed God the Son, and today God reveals Himself as God the Spirit. As leaders, we don't have to settle long-standing debates; rather, we must ask the Lord to teach us how to connect with our culture and communicate Christ creatively and effectively, regardless of how fast the world is changing.

It is not how clever we are but how Christ-centered we are that will result in souls being saved and disciples becoming soul-winners.

Many years ago I concluded that the center of Scripture is Jesus Christ. Jesus is the reason for the revelation of Scripture, so that all people might be saved from their sins. We're called to preach a Christ-centered Gospel. Jesus, the ultimate image and illustration, is the picture to be fastened in the minds of our listeners. And look at the imagery associated with Jesus! His life is a treasure trove of pictures and stories so vast that, even if you preached for a thousand years, you could not mine the depths of it all. Just as Abraham learned that it is all about the wedding, we need to comprehend that it is all about Jesus and His bride.

When the woman at the well wanted to talk about religious matters pertaining to the Word of God, Jesus directed her thoughts back to Himself, the Messiah (John 4:24-26). As a result, she came face-to-face with the realization that Jesus is the Son of God: "He is the Christ" (John 4:29).

The seventy preached the Kingdom of God and the Name of Jesus (Luke 10:9, 11, 17). Philip preached Jesus Christ to the Samaritans (Acts 8:5) and to the Ethiopian eunuch (Acts 8:35). Peter proclaimed peace through Jesus Christ to Cornelius and his household (Acts 10:36). The Apostle Paul declared to the Corinthians, "For I determined to know nothing among you except Jesus Christ and Him crucified," (1 Corinthians 2:2). The central thrust of the five-fold ministry of the church is the maturing of the Body of Jesus Christ (Ephesians 4:11-16). Clearly, Jesus is not simply an issue in evangelistic preaching; He is the main issue in our world today. He is the only way to God the Father.

As networkers, we need to demonstrate Jesus in creative ways that place Him centrally in the minds of the people we touch. After all, our networks are not about ourselves or our organizations or our churches or our denominations. Our networks are all about lifting Jesus higher—about fulfilling what is in His heart and in His heart alone. The picture of Christ that we present should not be clouded by Christianity. By this I mean that Christ, not religion, is the greatest magnet in the world today. He draws people to Himself as we lift Him higher and higher. It is not how clever we are but how Christ-centered we are that will result in souls being saved and disciples becoming soul-winners.

In the spring of 2009, I attended the graduation ceremonies at a renowned Christian seminary in the United States to witness an earned Doctorate being conferred on a friend's son. The commencement speaker was a professor from another well-known seminary, who proceeded to give the most embarrassing gospel presentation I've ever heard—and I have heard a lot of them. To begin his presentation, the professor made condescending references to the faculty behind him. Next, he assured the graduating class that they would not remember anything about his message. He proceeded to speak without referring to a biblical text or quoting a single scripture over the next forty minutes.

His title was the "Three B's," but he did not connect three B's to anything having to do with ministry. Instead, he launched into a commentary on American history, evidently not taking into consideration the fact that 40 percent of the class was from outside of the United States. (My friend and his son are from India.) He went on to cast one of America's founding fathers in a negative light and contrast him to a well-known contemporary. Both men were famously guilty of adultery, but the presenter described the founding father as a disgusting leader and the contemporary leader as an angel. No Scripture was provided to bring balance, clarity, or even the smallest bit of proof to support his shaky premise.

If what I heard at the start was surprising, it paled in comparison to the professor's shocking conclusions. For his last point, he stated that his third "B" stood for "Bodily Function," which led to a ten-minute reading from a children's fable in order to explain how a person becomes an agent of change.

This man's lack of biblical communication and failure to recognize the DNA of his audience was all the more embarrassing to me because I knew how hard my friend's son had worked, even to the point of making a transcontinental commute, to earn his Doctorate. I trust that this educator will be proved wrong; his words will be remembered for years, and this group of graduates will respond by doing the exact opposite of his example.

This was just one presentation, but I am noticing a trend among preachers who—rightly so—recognize that the communication chasm has widened enormously over the last two decades. They observe correctly that a common knowledge about the Bible does not exist in this culture any more. Older listeners are Gutenbergers (think: printing press), but younger listeners are Googlers (think: Internet giant). The information explosion has given these Googlers a different world view than the Gutenbergers and has driven them further away from any Gospel truth. But here's where these preachers, who otherwise perceive rightly, go wrong: they resort to shameful tricks and techniques to grab the attention of Googlers, even when it's at the expense of the Gutenbergers, the Gospel, and good manners.

It is true that whether we were born among the Googlers or the Gutenbergers, we have to move from misconnection and miscommunication to influence and impact in the hearts of our listeners. And of course, the closer we are to an age group, the faster we can cross the chasm of communication to that group. But if anyone ever told you that preparing powerful, creative presentations is easy, then he or she does not comprehend the contemporary obstacles that communicators face today.

Growth is what success is all about. Change is inevitable, but growth is optional. We have to be willing to grow as communicators in a rapidly changing world, where the attention spans of most people are shrinking and the power of concentration has been devalued. The age of rhetoric is dead. Too many speech teachers describe speaking as a medium of words rather than a medium of sight and sound which happens to use words. Reading speeches will not work. If people's minds are not debating halls but picture galleries, then we must create presentations that communicate in living color.

How do we do this? By using our sanctified imagination. Creativity is the product of imagination. For the networker, imagination creates a bridge between the past and the present.

Imagination isn't fantasy; it's vastly different. If you have ever been to Disney World in Orlando, Florida, you know that four very different theme parks are located on the massive Disney property. Fantasy is the Magic Kingdom—the world of Tinkerbell and Mickey Mouse. Imagination is EPCOT, where visitors explore new technologies, innovations, and the cultures of the world.

Imagination arouses faith in God and His Word. Imagination makes history come alive. It is one of the strongest allies we have in the effort to change lives forever. We cannot see the thoughts of God; they are hidden from us. God revealed those thoughts through the life of Jesus. Jesus became both the outward visual and vocal expressions of the inward thoughts of God. By helping others to see Jesus, we can lead them to an understanding of the thoughts and truths of God and a recognition of the difference Jesus Christ can make in their lives.

For networkers, imagination puts flesh and clothes on ideas and facts. It makes the unknown known and the unseen seen. The imaginative mind sees the difference between facts and ideas and recognizes how they can be brought together in a single presentation.

Steve Jobs, one of the greatest inventors of all time, once said that creativity is the ability to connect things. Master networkers are connectors. Just as a master carpenter knows how to pull together blueprints, wood, brick and nails in order to build a house, so the networker must know how to tie together the various parts of a meaningful message to form a powerful presentation.

In a famous U.S. court case that was recently dramatized in a movie, the inventor of the intermittent windshield wiper defended himself against corporate engineers who stole his idea. They claimed he used materials that were already in existence and therefore did not invent their use. In his defense, the inventor called for a book to be read. He stated to the judge that although each word of the book was common, the meaning of the words put together was the result of the author's creativity. Yes, the inventor had used the common building-blocks of engineering, but he had used them to create something new, and he won his case.

We must engage our creativity to connect people to a mission greater than themselves. In doing so they not only become better people; they achieve more because they are part of a net that works.

As networkers, we must creatively imagine a world that is filled with men and women in sync, working together within various systems in the Body of Christ in order to achieve goals of significant value that could never be achieved separately. Then, as we develop our presentations to share with various leaders—whether in person or on a conference call, in a congregational setting or a small or large group—we must employ a creativity that is capable of harnessing the attention of the men and women to whom we are casting our vision, using common words, thoughts, and technologies as our building blocks.

Creativity is hard work, but it's worth the effort. Without it we will either bore our listeners with dry words or offend them with bells and whistles that have no substance. Each audience is unique; they don't see the world as other people see it but as *they* see it. Sometimes, we assume that the world is the way we speak it and that reality matches the metaphors that we live by. The key to effective, creative communication isn't our world view; it's theirs. We must understand how our listeners imagine or view their world. Without true communication, there can be no real connection.

Our sacred responsibility is to have a biblically-guided imagination that allows us to cross the bridge between where we are and where our listeners are, between the biblical past and the contemporary present, in order to cast a vision that inspires them to believe God for great things. The danger lies in the fact that our minds serve as a filter or paradigm through which we must bring the accurate message of Scripture to the arena of ideas. That's why we need a *sanctified* imagination and a mind fully set upon God and His Word.

If we're going to be leaders that people respect and want to follow, then we've got to be able to communicate effectively and imaginatively so that people know where we're going. We must engage our creativity to cast vision in ways that draw others to want to share that vision and come alongside us.

Creativity in Connecting Relationships

Networkers are connectors. We engage our creativity to connect words, ideas, pictures, and technology to build creative presentations that instruct and challenge and inspire. But the most important things that we connect are people. A network cannot exist without people. There is no point in tying knots if that does not mean connecting people for a greater cause. We must engage our creativity to connect people to a mission greater than themselves. In doing so they not only become better people; they achieve more because they are part of a net that works.

The late Adrian Rogers used to say, "A person wrapped up in themselves makes an awfully small package." That's one thing the Billion Soul Network is *not* about. BSN is not about small packages and small people. Our view is that there's never a problem too big to solve, only too many small people trying to solve it. It's important that we understand this if we're going to achieve something of real value and lasting significance.

In an earlier chapter I introduced the idea, "no knots, no net." This creative connection between knot-making and networking came to me in the summer of 2010, when I was ministering with Pastor Barry Clardy, senior pastor at Princeton Pike Church of God in Cincinnati, Ohio. We were driving along in the car and Pastor Clardy made a statement that stirred my imagination. "I am a knot-maker," he said. "I tie knots in Cincinnati." He understood the root of real networking. His word-picture caught my attention then and it still does to this day.

So, how do we go about tying knots? How do we creatively engage people and help them take the necessary steps to join us on the journey of doing greater things together?

1. We connect socially.

First of all, we connect socially. It is important for us to spend time with the right people in the right places in order to become the right person. I've been fortunate to travel a lot over the past thirty years; but in the last few years I have made it a priority to travel great distances to spend time with only one person, so that (1) I may become a better individual, (2) I might have the opportunity to connect that person with other people, and (3) I might connect that person to a greater vision, so he or she can grow in the grace and knowledge of Jesus Christ.

It's vital that we connect socially. Not too long ago, a group of eight Australian church leaders were in Orlando. I live about an hour away, so I drove over to have dinner and spend a little time with them. Then, I turned around and went back home.

You might think, "That is not very far to travel to have a meeting with a distinguished group who came all the way from Australia." It is true that driving to Orlando is not a big deal, but what about traveling half way around the world? In this group of eight was one key leader who I had first sought out by traveling all the way to his home country just to have lunch with him. That was not unusual for me. I have traveled to distant continents for a day meeting only to turn around and fly home the next day.

Some people might consider this practice a waste of time, energy and money. But, I'm a connector and a knot-maker. I understand that there are mountains of ministry that God has raised up around the world, and I strive to connect them to help fulfill the Great Commission. That's what a networker does. That's who a networker is.

I do not know of any networkers who are islands unto themselves. A networker engages people where they are, so they can connect with others for that greater purpose.

2. We connect skillfully.

Successful networkers not only connect socially; they connect skillfully. Think about it. If we're going to spend thirty minutes in an automobile with a key leader, wouldn't it be important for us to have an understanding of who the individual is so we can engage him or her with specific questions, and not just talk about the weather? We need to make an effort to learn something of value so that when we get out of the car we can say, "Now that was worth the trip. That was worth my time and energy."

Another aspect of connecting skillfully is that as we get to know people socially, we discover their talents, abilities, and skills. Then, when we're working to connect one person with another, we know what skill sets each person brings to the table. We know who is knowledgeable about a particular idea and who has mastered a particular method. We're able to connect the right people together so that the work of the Lord can flourish.

Connecting skillfully also involves understanding how to navigate and communicate. Everybody does not have the same worldview. Everybody is not at the same place in life and is not ready to connect in the same way. It's important that we have a good sense of timing as to when to connect one person with another. Sometimes too fast is too soon. Sometimes too slow is a missed opportunity. In baseball, a foul ball is the result of poor timing. But using the same bat and the same ball, we can hit one over the fence if our timing is right.

When I was in Indonesia for a Billion Soul Summit in July 2012, I watched an Indonesian leader saddle up next to a renowned North American leader. The two men hadn't known one another before the summit. The conversation was about connecting an Indonesian seminary with a North American school. It was just a brief conversation, but I know that the Indonesian leader was disappointed with the outcome. I wasn't surprised. From my perspective, it was much too fast and too soon for there to have been a positive outcome. It would have been wiser for that Indonesian leader to connect first with the person who had known the American leader for twenty years and who had brought him to the summit in the first place (me). I could have told him that the timing wasn't right and helped him make a more skillful connection.

3. We connect spiritually.

In addition to connecting socially and skillfully, we need to be sure we engage our creativity with people spiritually. After all, we're not networking for business; we're networking for the Great Commission. We're not networking for money; we're networking for ministry—for missions around the world. We must network spiritually. I believe the Lord wants to lead us to the right people in the right place at the right time, and He will put great people in our path when we need them.

The Lord wants to lead us to the right people in the right place at the right time, and He will put great people in our path when we need them.

Dr. Bill Bright once told me, "When the Lord is putting an idea in your heart, the Lord is also putting that same idea in other people's hearts, and only the Holy Spirit knows how to get all those people together to achieve that idea. A God-sized idea requires more than you. A God-sized idea requires lots of people getting in sync together, synergistically serving one another to achieve a God-sized goal."

There have been many times when I've seen the divine hand of God put people in my path so that I might "grow and go," not "dry and die." Networking must be a spiritual endeavor. We must connect spiritually with God and with one another.

4. We connect systematically.

You and I need to live our lives and develop our networks in a systematic way. We need to plan ahead and ask the Lord to give us direction as to how we are to go. We need to be "actionary," not reactionary.

Recently, I convinced a key leader to serve as a co-chair in the Billion Soul Network. I knew how to communicate our vision to him because I had, over time, developed a system—a way of going about my networking business. I didn't have to go back and re-invent the wheel or develop a new template for communicating with him. I was systematic in making this important connection.

5. We connect successfully.

As networkers, we need to remember: Great dreams inspire great people. We attract who we are, not what we want. Favor is better than labor. As we embrace our creativity and learn how to connect with others socially, skillfully, spiritually, and systematically, we will become successful knot-makers. Our lives and ministries will become the rope that God uses to tie the knot of Kingdom purpose. Ultimately, His sovereign hands will pull the drawstrings, revealing the great net that has been created—the global net that He will use to bring in this last-day harvest.

In the process, we will become the answer to Christ's prayer in John 17:18-23: "As You sent me into the world, I also have sent them into the world ... The glory which you have given Me I have given to them, that they may be one, just as We are one; I in them and You in Me, that they may be perfected in unity, so that the world may know that You sent Me, and loved them, even as You have loved Me."

6

Explore Your Core

If we're going to develop a net that works, we need to explore our core—that is, we need to consider, incorporate, and apply certain core values in our lives. We need to move our hearts and minds in five key areas in order to become leaders who can network with others at all levels for the higher purpose of moving the Church closer to fulfilling the Great Commission.

The Movement of the Networker

As master networkers, our effectiveness will depend largely upon our ability to move from being competitors with other leaders to becoming collaborators with them; from being critics of others to becoming complimenters of others; from being complainers to becoming connectors. We must also move from being men and women who are mere day-dreamers to becoming true visionaries. Finally, we must move from being workers who are self-centered and focused on our own ministries to becoming leaders who are centered on Christ and His purposes in the world.

Let's look at each of these critical movements more closely.

1. Moving from Competitor to Collaborator

Let's begin with moving from competitor to collaborator. It is important for us to understand that we're not trying to outdo somebody else. We're trying to achieve something by working together that could never be achieved individually.

I've highlighted this before, but I want to bring it home more clearly here. Competition may be good for economic growth, but collaboration creates an environment where people can share their ideas and their resources. People must be allowed to believe that their thoughts matter and their ideas will be heard. The reason so many pastors and ministers are not currently networking in their communities is because of the spirit of competition. It is what tears down networks rather than building them up.

The reason so many pastors and ministers are not currently networking in their communities is because of the spirit of competition. It is what tears down networks rather than building them up.

Let me give you an example. Let's say a pastor moves to a new metropolitan area, and he spends the first year or two developing relationships with key people in his ministry and maybe with others outside his church. In his third year he decides to establish a Christian school. Now, there's nothing wrong with a Christian school. There is nothing wrong with equipping our children and our young people. What if a Christian school already exists in the neighborhood, however? As soon as he opens a new Christian school near an existing Christian school, he becomes a competitor to that first school. It may not be his goal to be a competitor; but when he chooses to develop his own school rather than consult and collaborate with the school that is already there, he puts himself in competition.

The same thing often happens when a pastor or a denomination decides to plant a new church. When a pastor plants a church in an area where other active churches already exist, regardless of whether it was meant to happen or not, competition sets in. What we ought to do is strategically consider where there are no churches and plant churches there first! We must develop a Great Commission mindset and Great Commission spirit that challenges others to think this way too.

2. Moving from Critic to Complimenter

We should also move from being a critic to being a complimenter. For every criticism you speak, give three compliments. Sometimes it's easier for us to see and point out what is not working than to see and point out what is working. It is easier to find what is bad than to articulate what is good. I can promise you that critics don't have big networks. Critics repel people away from them rather than compel people to come to them.

Have you ever noticed that when two pastors from the same city get together for lunch, they tend to spend most of their time criticizing another pastor in town? Rather than spending time getting to know the third pastor and inviting him to come to lunch *with* them, they choose to have him *for* lunch with their unkind words.

It is important that we, in the very essence of our lives, choose to focus on the positive instead of on the negative, the good rather than the bad. That does not mean that we should bury our heads in the sand and ignore the problems of our day. Rather, we should remember that our goal is to develop a network that works. We must leave criticism at the door and show the way, rather than criticize those who have not yet found the way. A positive, winning mindset that focuses on what is good in a person, a church, or a ministry can make all the difference.

Several years ago, I had to endure a series of criticisms from some people who chose to attack me personally. They did their best to derail our ministry. It was a most difficult time for me and it lasted for two long, grueling years. There were times I wondered if it would ever end. I bring this up not to relive the past, but to demonstrate to you that I had to choose each day how I was going to respond. From that day until now, I never answered the critics or responded to the cynics. Even when these people chose to write letters to certain leaders to attack me in print, by the grace of God, I chose to climb higher in my heart and actions and rise above it all.

The temptation in such circumstances is to get down and wrestle in the mud to "teach those people a thing or two." Yet, at the end of day, time is wasted, lives are not changed and the vision is not fulfilled. Even though the individuals who criticized me never made things right, I chose not to allow their bad spirit to corrupt my spirit.

3. Moving from Complainer to Connector

If you say, "That's not easy," then you are right in your conclusion. However, our gracious Lord gives us the strength to follow Him on the high road!

As networkers, we must choose to connect rather than complain. When we get hit with small thinking, we must step up higher in our own thinking and actions.

Don't complain about your circumstances. This whole book is about connecting, not complaining. It's about getting the right people together to achieve something they could never do by themselves. Complaining never mobilized an audience. Complaining never put the Cross on the roof of the world. Complaining never built great kingdoms. Complaining never established a great company.

As networkers, we must choose to connect rather than complain. When we get hit with small thinking, we must step up higher in our own thinking and actions. We must move from the low level of day-dreaming (seeing only what's in front of us day-to-day) to the highest level of Christ-centered vision. Negativism may sell but it does not save!

4. Moving from Casual to Causal

How do we do this? How do we rise above the day-dream and move toward a Christ-centered vision for our network and ministry? The reality is, life is lived in seasons. The ocean has ebbs and flows. Nature has its chain of life. Economies have cycles of growth. Vision, too, has a process of success.

On a recent weekend, I was fortunate to minister with Pastor Walter Harvey, senior pastor of Parklawn Assembly in Milwaukee, Wisconsin. Parklawn is one of the fastest-growing congregations in the United States. During our lunch conversation, he shared with me the following powerful and insightful twelve-step visionary process:

a) **Birth Date:** *The vision must be born from within.* Your vision must a have a birthdate, a beginning date. You must know that *you know* that the vision is from the Lord and that He has assigned you to fulfill it.

b) **Subscribe:** *The vision has to be owned.* The leader reads and studies all the elements relating to the vision. Until you take ownership of that which has been given to you, you will never move from a man's day-dream to a God-sized vision.

c) **Inscribe:** *The vision must be written.* The greatest visions are written into short, pungent statements. Short does not mean shallow. Until you are able to write it down in concise wording, your vision will not be clear to others. Write it down so you can run with it.

d) **Describe:** *The vision must be shared with key partners.* Until the God-vision is shared with others, you will not be able to build and broaden a net that works.

e) **Prescribe:** *The vision must have steps for the involvement of partners.* You need to develop many different kinds of on-ramps to the highway of the vision. People come to a project from different angles; they need different doors to walk through to achieve divine fulfillment in their lives.

f) **Persecution:** *The vision will be attacked by others with different agendas.* Sooner or later the visionary and the vision come under attack. I am not sure that you can prevent it. Even the best-prepared cannot discern the wolves from the sheep every time.

g) **Betrayal:** *The vision will be betrayed by some who claim to be allies.* There is something deep about this. The greatest battles are not fought outside of our circle but inside our circle. When you are in doubt about someone, be careful what you say and do.

h) **Death:** *The vision must die to be powerful.* This is the most painful time in a visionary's life. You may end up feeling all alone and wonder if you, and the vision, will live again. Start climbing out of the grave! Keep on doing what the Lord has commanded you to do. The greatest conqueror of criticism is success!

i) **Resurrection:** *The vision will become more powerful than before.* Death and resurrection brings greater influence and more results. Your critics will dance at your apparent death; but when the Lord resurrects you and the vision, it will demonstrate the power and plan of Christ to them and the world.

j) **Provision:** *The vision has greater provision than ever.* People of provision who were watching in the past will begin to give generously for the vision to be fulfilled in this generation. The higher the respect, the higher the revenue!

k) **Speaks For Itself:** *The vision now speaks for itself.* Now people are talking about what the vision is accomplishing, without the visionary leader doing all of the communicating. Testimonies come after the test. When you pass the vision test, people will begin talking about what the Lord is doing, even when you are not talking about it at all.

l) **Multiplication:** *The vision has moved from addition to multiplication.* All future planning is built upon multiplication-focused thinking and execution for compounding results. This is the time when visionaries commit the rest of their lives to reproducing instead of just producing. Your every assignment is now viewed through this lens of acceptance and application.

I encourage you to take the time to ponder and pray over these twelve steps. After all, the greatest visionary leader of all time, Jesus Christ, was born, persecuted, died, resurrected, and multiplied His vision to live eternally!

5. Moving from Self-Centered to the Center

Great networkers don't focus on themselves. They don't seek a position. Rather, they explore their core and take the next step: they learn how to mobilize and minister from the middle. They learn how to articulate vision from the middle, lead from the middle, and connect from the middle. What do I mean by the middle? To be great networkers, it is important that we develop a circumference to our lives, recognizing that there are people at all levels of leadership who encircle us on all sides. As networkers, we are in the middle of that circle. Our goal is to develop the skills that will enable us to reach out in every direction to connect, support, and encourage these people from the middle, challenging them to catch our vision and believe God for the extraordinary in their lives.

The Middle of the Networker

You may be the founder of your ministry or the originator of your movement; but to be a master networker, you must understand that the very essence of networking is leading people from the middle. We're not so much leading from out front, as in a parade, or from the top down, as in a pyramid; we're leading from the center of a circle of relationships, connecting people, connecting ideas, and connecting goals in a dynamic and systematic way.

In the Billion Soul Network we purposely don't talk about having a chairman or a president; we talk about having co-chairs. Currently there are over 225 Billion Soul co-chairs, each with equivalent leadership responsibilities in their regions or areas of expertise. We are neither "in front" nor "in back" of each other. We're neither "above" nor "below" one another. Rather, we're leadership peers, working together to achieve the fulfillment of the Great Commission.

As you develop your network, think in terms of developing the circumference of your life and your relationships. This is the key to successful networking and exponential growth toward the common goal. Envision yourself not as out front or on top, but in the middle. Remember, great people follow great vision. Personally, I envision my life as that of a networker who is able to network on several different levels. These levels continue to develop and mature over time.

I have learned that it is important to invest in people, to sow into their lives, and to cultivate relationships in our communities and beyond in order to extend our circumference. I call this navigating among the various key people that God has put into our lives. Many times this means reaching out to leaders who are more well-known or have greater influence than we do. How do we navigate and lead in such situations? We lead from the middle.

1. Leading Up

There are three distinct ways that we can lead from the middle. The first is to "lead up." For the networker, this means recognizing, supporting, and serving those who are top leaders or influencers in our organization, denomination, or the Body of Christ as a whole. Even though we may be leaders ourselves, we want to demonstrate a very strong servant's heart toward these key leaders.

We can best serve those in leadership by demonstrating that we are, first of all, leaders of ourselves. That means doing everything with as much personal excellence as possible. It means showing up polished, prepared, and with the right perspective to our meetings. It means demonstrating that we know our subject matter, that we've done our homework and research, that we're well-equipped for the task and that we've developed strong networking leadership skills.

Never show up unprepared and waste another leader's time. As I often say, "It may only be a minute, but eternity is in it." You may have a more expensive watch than I do, but you don't have any more time than I do! If you schedule a meeting, show up on time for that meeting. If you see that you're going to be late, call the leader and say so. Respect for others goes a long way in establishing credibility.

"Leading up" also requires us to have a good sense of timing. When we're dealing with influential leaders, we need to know when we should push forward and when we should back off. Unfortunately, many people can't tell the difference between the two and they end up alienating instead of communicating.

Finally, we "lead up" as networkers by being willing to do what others are not willing to do. I've often said that there are times when we shout, there are times when we stand, and there are times when we stoop. Many leaders are not willing to stoop and serve; therefore, they will never be able to lead great networks from the middle.

Jesus said that when you are asked to go one mile, you offer to go the second mile. Master networkers are not first milers. We are second milers.

Jesus said that when you are asked to go one mile, you offer to go the second mile. Master networkers are not first milers. We are second milers. We demonstrate service and sacrifice, expending whatever extra time and energy is necessary to make sure things within the network are done and done well. In my experience, there's a lot of traffic on the first mile, but there's not much traffic on the second mile. The second mile is the victory mile; it is the blessed mile. Many leaders never discover this victory and blessing because they never make it to that level.

I learned a long time ago when I was working in my denominational headquarters that I wanted to be the best I could be. I wanted to be as prepared as I could possibly be. I became a go-to person when ideas were being shared or when things needed to be done. I am often contacted by leaders from across the country and around the world when they want another leader's phone number or when they need to know if another leader is still living in a certain city or working with a particular ministry. I can't tell you how many people see me as the go-to person for locating other people in the Body of Christ. I take this as a great compliment.

All of us need to become go-to people, whether it's within our organization, among pastors in our city, or beyond. We need to be better tomorrow than we are today—to continue to "grow up" so that we might "go up." If we have not grown into a higher leadership role but find ourselves leading beyond our current capabilities, we will cause stress to ourselves and stress to the people around us, and our circle will not become stronger but weaker.

It's very important that we not try to "manage" our lives and the lives of others. We're not called to manage but to lead. We're called to demonstrate networking leadership from the middle.

2. Leading Across

The second way to lead from the middle is to lead *across* our circumference. Some people think a network is made up of similar people working in unity. I see it more as diverse people working in harmony. We all have different parts to sing, but it is still the same song: finishing the Great Commission. When we lead across, we harmonize.

How do we do this? We do this by seeking to lighten the loads of our peers and finding ways to add value to their lives and ministries. In the Billion Soul Network, these peers are our fellow co-chairs. Perhaps we recommend good resources that we've come across. If we've done some writing, we give our books away. We introduce them to some of the other great people we know, in order to expand their circumference, expose them to new ideas, and give them and their ministries greater impact for the long run.

We made an important point earlier: The goal is to move from being competitors to collaborators. Another way to say this is that we need to be about *completing* fellow leaders, not *competing* with them. If you develop a spirit of completing, then people will want to get close to you. If other leaders understand that your desire is to complete something, rather than compete against something or someone, then they are more likely to go with you not only the extra mile but the full distance.

Essentially, we're talking about being a friend. As networkers, we should go out of our way to develop friendships. I challenge people to develop a friendship every week. Get more and more acquainted with acquaintances. Reach out the right hand of fellowship. Sow a little bit into somebody's life and you will reap eternal dividends. Jesus taught that those who are friendly will have friends. He also taught that we must be careful of the standard we choose. The standard by which we judge others is the same standard that will be applied to us.

Here are a few additional keys to leading across in your network:

- Avoid politics—politics in your organization, politics among pastors, politics in your denomination. Choose to rise above politics, and you will challenge those in your circle of influence to rise above it as well.
- Do not have any part in gossip. Gossipers do not build networks; they do not build people. If the people you attract are gossipers that is no compliment to you. Squelch out gossip instead of participating in it and others will follow your lead.
- When you're in a conversation, at a committee meeting, in a conference call, or when you have called together key people in your network to work on a problem, let the best solution win. Let the best idea remain on the table. Get to the place in your life where you don't care who comes up with the idea, how the project gets done or who gets the credit.
- Apologize when you make a mistake or do something wrong.
- Don't try to present a persona of perfectionism.
- Don't pretend to know it all. When someone asks you about something, be willing to tell them you don't know. They will believe you the next time when you *do* know.

- Complete the information loop. In other words, keep everyone informed from the start of a process to the end. If you send e-mails to a group of people, for example, make sure all the same people stay in the chain and get all the responses. Click "reply all" to complete the circle of communication. I see far too many leaders inadvertently or mistakenly not copying the right people in e-mails, keeping critical people out of the loop.

- To be a master networker, you must continuously go around your circle to make sure that every key person in the circumference of your life and ministry is up-to-date and knows what's going on.

- When a task or project is complete, send a simple note that says, "Done." Help close the chapter in the minds of those involved.

3. Leading Down

In addition to leading up and leading across, master networkers must learn to lead down. This means leading those who look up to us as their leaders and influencers. It's not that we're *looking down* on people, as if we're better than they are. That's not the way we view people in the Billion Soul Network; it's not the way we view other pastors and leaders. Rather, when we lead down, we're seeking to encourage others and lift them up so that they can reach their full potential in Christ. In the process, we're creating the kind of environment that is most conducive for successful networking. In such an environment, people are more willing to ask questions and go above and beyond to make sure their part of the job is done with the greatest of care and excellence.

Our goal is to develop teams—a spine of networkers that is the backbone of all that we do and accomplish. We've said it before: leaders cannot live on islands. We need other people to help us achieve a common vision. A leadership team is always more effective than just one person. There is only one "1" in the number 1,000,000,000. The rest are zeros. The number "1" by itself is not enough to accomplish anything of global significance. We need to be willing to add value to those in front of us and behind us, to those above us and below us, in order to develop a circumference that is capable of changing the world.

We need talented people and diverse skills on every level of our network. This doesn't mean that we need complicated and cumbersome systems and hierarchies; on the contrary, as we said in Chapter 3, we want to develop networks that are lean and mean. Nevertheless, it will take a lot of different people with a lot of different skill sets working together to achieve something of greater significance than any one person could do on their own.

We need to be willing to add value to those in front of us and behind us, to those above us and below us, in order to develop a circumference that is capable of changing the world.

The Model of the Networker

Years ago, when I was a teenager living in Mobile, Alabama, our church relocated. The new sanctuary was built and the time came to lay down sod and put in bushes and shrubbery. I watched as our pastor got out there on the front lawn of the church, down on his hands and knees, to help lay the sod with the other men from the church. That day, he demonstrated servant leadership. Without saying a word, he was communicating to me and to all the men around him, "I'm not too good to get dirty. I'm not too good to put my hands in the mud." Because of his willingness to get dirty and work hard, the men around him were inspired to do their best as well.

Though this pastor has long retired and never built a network, he showed on that day that he was the true leader of the church. He chose to lead from the middle. He didn't have a sod business, he didn't have a nursery, his job description didn't include manual labor; but he decided to get out there anyway. He chose to demonstrate what it was to stoop, to serve, to connect various men around him to accomplish a very simple but meaningful project. His example challenged me and it continues to challenge me to this day.

Networker, I encourage you to explore your core. Don't be a critic or a complainer. Don't compete with other leaders; choose instead to *complete* them. Consider ways to develop your life's circumference and make the conscious decision to connect with others from the middle. Lead up, across, and down to connect people and tie relationship knots that make the value of your network worth much more than the sum of its parts. In time, you will be able to look back and see hundreds of knots that have been tied and relationships that have been cultivated, woven into a net capable of bringing in a greater harvest of souls than you ever imagined.

7

Equip Your Circle

The stronger your inner circle, the stronger your network will become. A chain is only as strong as its weakest link. All of us have known leaders we thought would rise to greatness, only to see them settle in weakness. We've also known leaders we thought were weak who turned out to be stronger than we expected. Often the difference comes down to one thing: proper equipping.

If we properly equip our inner circle of leadership relationships, the ripple effect that will result from having stronger leaders will build momentum for our cause and create movement into the future. If your movement is not moving, it's not a movement, it's a monument! Too many leaders convince themselves that they're making progress, when in fact they haven't moved at all; they haven't created a single ripple. If we want our networks to grow in influence and impact—if we want to create a movement, not a monument—then we must be able to equip, teach, and develop those the Lord has put in our path.

Our Net Worth is in Our Network

The most important thing we must teach and develop in those leaders within our spheres of influence is correct thinking. Now, correct thinking is extremely hard work. It's not something that comes naturally. It's not taught in schools; I don't know of a university anywhere in the world where a person can get a degree in thinking. Therefore, it is up to us as master networkers to learn for ourselves, and then teach those around us, three levels of thinking and training that will ensure that we build a movement that moves and a network that works: the right purpose, the right process, the right product, and the right paradigms.

The Right Purpose

In order to teach others to think with the right purpose, we need to have a clear understanding of what that purpose is. This statement represents the first level of correct thinking: *Our net worth is born out of our network.* Personally, I don't measure my net worth by my material assets but by my relational assets. The personal relationships that Christ has given to me are my greatest assets in this life and in the life to come. That's a true statement for every believer and certainly for every networker.

At the Billion Soul Network, we have worked hard to make our purpose crystal-clear. As I've already articulated, the purpose of Billion Soul is to synergize the efforts of key Christian leaders around the world with the goal of doubling the size of the Church. Our purpose is to make it hard for someone to live on Planet Earth and not hear an adequate witness of the Gospel of Jesus Christ. We believe that doubling the size of the Church and increasing the number of churches worldwide puts us in a position to finish the Great Commission in our lifetime. How successful we are in reaching this goal depends upon the quality of the networking relationships we build across the world.

1. The right purpose determines the plan.

Only by allowing the right purpose to direct your thinking will you come up with the right plan for achieving it. At Billion Soul, we have kept our clearly-defined purpose in the forefront of our thinking as we have developed our plans for achieving the goal. If we had a different purpose in mind, we would most certainly have a different plan! Whenever I am around others in my circle of influence, I make every effort to share our purpose with clarity and confidence. Leaders who communicate uncertainty about their ministry's purpose or plan do not motivate other people to get involved.

2. The right plan directs the path.

The path that you take going forward in your network is the direct result of the plan you have developed, which is determined by the purpose you have defined. This is what I call "creating a leaning domino." The right purpose creates the "weight" that leads to the right plan, which leads to the right path, and so on. You create movement in your network that people can see and feel and they want to become a part of it.

Leaders who communicate uncertainty about their ministry's purpose or plan do not motivate other people to get involved.

The Right Process

In addition to having the right purpose, we need to have the right process. One leads to the other; different purpose, different process.

3. The right path delineates the process.

Once you know your path, you can go about it in a specific way. In my position as a networker, I spend a lot of time on airplanes. Over time I have developed a process that I go through to get ready for each flight. I have often shared that process with others who travel less frequently. For example, I get everything I need into one carry-on bag so that I never have to worry about checked luggage. In order to teach and develop the inner circle of relationships in your life, let others step into your world and see how you process information, how you process instruction, and how you process various aspects of your life.

4. The right process develops the procedures.

Procedures are set up to fulfill the process. They move us forward. They're like the wheels on an automobile. You can have all the blueprints, parts, and know-how you need to build the vehicle, but unless you put wheels on it, it will not roll.

What are the procedures that are going to move you toward your goal? I have come to believe that the best procedures for achieving success are often the simplest and most straightforward. Complicated procedures create bottlenecks that cause you to struggle and hold up progress. If there's a bottleneck in your process, review your procedures and remove it.

5. The right procedures dictate the practices.

The policy manual of a networking organization should be prepared through the lens of the vision of the network: with broad strokes, followed by specifics—not the other way around. Once you have the purpose, plan, path, process, and procedures down, then you can say, "This is the way we do it: A, B, C, D, E, F, G." You can put into place the right practices that will make your network operate smoothly and effectively.

I am raising two lovely daughters, and I have taught them from the early days of their adoption that it's not just practice that makes perfect; it is the *right* kind of practice that makes perfect. Often people fail to fine-tune the way they go about their life and their practice, and therefore the outcome of their life is not very successful. As networkers, we need to have the right practices and be willing to fine-tune them from time to time.

6. The right practices direct the partners.

Once you have a policy and specific practices in place, then you can direct your partners, those people and organizations that have agreed to work with you, toward one or more of your networking goals. Setting up certain ways of doing things that everyone can follow is important, because different people have different approaches to getting things done. Some people look at a mountain and immediately say, "Let's take the mountain." Other people say, "Well, I know a better way to take the mountain." Others step back, look at the whole mountain range, and say, "Let's think about this a little longer." If the practices of your network are already identified and communicated, your partners will know the way to go and everyone will be on the same page.

The Right Product

The great 18th century evangelist Jonathan Wesley once said that he was "writing for the movement." In other words, he was spending his time in inspirational and instructional writing in order to help others fulfill their divine calling. I believe that is what the Lord has had me doing recently with my time. Today's global Church needs to develop resources and tools to help pastors, leaders, and believers around the world grow in their lives and fulfill their callings.

7. The right partners deliver the product.

What is the product of your network? It could be shared resources, strategic world summits, or the creation of new materials such as a book or a training series. The product could also be a more general outcome, such as synergized relationships, goal-setting, or strategic planning. At the Billion Soul Network, we always make sure that whatever a product generates, whether revenue or influence or goodwill, we share the results with our many partners. Our desire is to add value to everyone in our network.

A few years ago I wrote a book called *Gutenberg to Google: The Twenty Indispensable Laws of Communication*. I sent the electronic files to a dear friend and church leader in Nigeria. He took the files and, using the printing presses at the Nigerian Baptist Convention, published the book and put it up for sale there. We were able to split the proceeds, with half the money going to local church planting in Nigeria, and the other half going to grow the Billion Soul Network around the world. We chose to partner to deliver a product in a non-traditional way. I believe these kinds of non-traditional partnerships are a global wave of the future that is already moving across the earth.

The Mission Is Built into the Movement

Once we understand that our net worth is born out of our network, we can move on to the next level in our thinking and training within our inner circle: *The mission is built into the movement.*

Having a group of men and women who are ambitious and passionate about fulfilling the Great Commission is a good thing. It's even better when those men and women are multiplied so that they are no longer a group; they become a movement. I've heard a lot of talk in leadership circles in recent years about applying the multiplication process to church growth, but I have not seen much multiplication actually taking place. Yet, multiplication is exactly what we need to complete the Great Commission in our lifetime.

Think of the Pacific Ocean. It's more than 13,000 feet deep on average. If you were to drain all of the water out of it, you would end up with an empty basin so large that you could take all the continents of the earth and place them in there. Then you could get Asia a second time and put it on top. That's how big the Pacific Ocean is!

Having a group of people who are ambitious about fulfilling the Great Commission is a good thing. It's even better when those people are multiplied so that they are no longer a group; they become a movement.

Now, let's say you were given the assignment to refill the empty Pacific. How would you choose to do that? Would you try to refill it one drop at a time? How many drops of water do you think it would take? How long would you have to work at it? Forever! You would never live to see it to completion.

But what if you chose to double each amount that you put in? First you put in one drop. Then you doubled it and put in two drops. Then you doubled *that* and put in four drops. Then you doubled *that* and put in eight drops, then sixteen drops, then thirty-two drops, then sixty-four drops, and so on. Do you know that on the eightieth doubling, you would have refilled the entire Pacific? On the eighty-first doubling, you would have two Pacific Oceans. On the eighty-second doubling, you would have four! That is the power of multiplication. That is the power of a movement.

Great leaders are not known just for finishing things, but also for the things they start in their lives that continue after they're gone. They're not just little pebbles dropped into the water; they're great rocks that hit the water and cause a giant rippling effect. Unfortunately, most leaders do not produce much of a ripple and most movements do not end the way their founders intended. In fact, here's the typical cycle of a movement: The first generation generates. The second generation motivates. The third generation speculates. The fourth generation dissipates.

Generations have come and gone, yet the Great Commission is still not fulfilled. Movements have come and gone, yet we have still fallen far short of the goal. The average leader believes that his or her movement will not age or become the opposite of what it started out to be; and yet history tells us, almost without exception, that's exactly what happens. Consider the example of some of our great denominations. Once they were conservative and filled with vigor and vitality. Now they are liberal and gradually drying up and dying away.

I want to be the kind of leader whose impact on the world continues long after I'm gone. Every master networker should have the same goal—not for our own sakes, but for the sake of the vision and the mission God has given us. The question is, can a mission really be built into a sustainable movement? Can we really move from simple addition to exponential multiplication in the way we grow the Church? I believe it can, if we understand and apply these keys:

1. The mission compels the message.

Notice, it's not the message that compels the mission; the mission compels the message. The mission is for the glory of the Lord to cover the earth like the water covers the sea. The mission is for every boy, girl, man, and woman to have an adequate witness of the gospel of Jesus Christ. For that mission, we have a message that must get out to everyone. That's the goal. Anything short of that is not a God-sized vision.

I would even go a step further and say that any mission that seems to take the longest route to reach the goal is not God's plan. I believe the Lord desires for everyone to hear the Gospel as soon as possible. James E. Rolfing, a theologian of a different generation, said, "The Gospel is only good news if it gets there in time. If it did not get there in time, it was no news at all."

2. The message is carried by its members.

We are all ambassadors for Christ and members of His body. We are missionaries to the world. It is up to us to carry the message of God to all those who need to hear it. Fortunately, it's not a complicated message that only the greatest among us can carry. The late Adrian Rogers, one of the great preachers of modern times, said, "Once you've studied, simplify your message. Then, simplify it again. Then, when you get up and preach it, the people will call you profound."

The Billion Soul Network has a message and it is linked to the fulfillment of the Great Commission. The members of the network, the co-chairs, pastors, and leaders, carry that message into their own regions and spheres of influence.

3. The members commit to the methods.

The point is not to commit to just any methods, but to methods that are tried and true, methods that have been tested and can be trusted and methods that are simplistic and straight-forward. These are the methods that really work. Successful methods take the "think time" out of whatever is being done. We all lead busy lives. If we can help a busy person save time, we've added great value to his or her life. By equipping our circle with effective methods, we take the "think time" out of what they have to do, and that saves a lot of time.

4. The methods cause the multiplication.

This is an important step, because without a template there cannot be multiplication. Once you write and produce a book the first time, that book never has to be written again. You just reproduce it whenever you need it. Likewise, if you have a template for growing your network, you can share that template with others. Then, they can focus on multiplying the template and moving forward rather than rewriting the book.

This is why it's important that we identify the best methods in the Body of Christ today; not just any methods but the best methods. It doesn't matter if the method comes from your world region or someone else's world region. Many of the best methods are being developed in diverse places outside the Western Church in countries such as India, Indonesia, and the Fiji Islands. One of the main goals of the Billion Soul Network is to seek out and share the best methods and the best models of multiplication wherever they may be found.

5. The multiplication creates a movement.

Until you have multiplication factored into your network, you really do not have a movement. Our goal is not to grow the Church little by little. Our goal is to grow the Church exponentially.

Weeks before Dr. Bill Bright passed away he told me, "When I cease to be productive, when I cease to add value, I'm not interested in staying here any longer."

May this be our passion and purpose as well! As networkers, we want to be productive. We want to add value to the lives of others. We want to be multipliers and we want to teach those God has entrusted to us to be multipliers too. Let's choose to plant churches that are committed to planting other churches. Let's set a goal to equip ten pastors who can plant ten churches each, so we can have one hundred new churches. The more we can equip our circle to be multipliers, the more multiplication we can do.

6. The movement communicates the models.

It is one thing for us to have a methodology, but it is another thing for us to have models. Look at the models God has raised up around the world. I call them mountains of ministry. Many key pastors and leaders have learned to do things in certain ways that have proven to be extremely successful. As a result, they have developed massive global organizations. These are models to be learned. They are models to be applied to our networks and our lives.

7. The models continue the mission.

This step brings us full circle. It is important that we have systematic models of real ministry to incorporate into our network so that our efforts can be duplicated and multiplied and our mission can become a movement that flourishes and grows. After all, as we said before, our net worth is born out of our network. There is no way we can place a value on the network that God has given to us. We need to learn how to build our network into a movement and then work to strengthen and broaden it each and every day of our lives.

Synergistic Networking

The real strength, power, and energy of a network is in its synergy. Developing and cultivating synergy is critical for building a powerful, interpersonal network with a global outcome. The deeper the synergy, the wider and more effective the net will be. Unfortunately, many networks are all "house" and no "foundation." When we take the time to do the relational groundwork and build upon a strong synergistic base, our network will be able to go farther and higher than we ever imagined.

Developing and cultivating synergy is critical for building a powerful, interpersonal network with a global outcome.

"Synergy" comes from the Greek word *synergia*, meaning joint work and cooperative action. With synergy, the result is always greater than the sum of the parts. Synergy is created when things work in concert together to create an outcome that is in some way of more value than the sum total of the individual inputs.

The English prefix *syn-* and its variant *sym-* are derived from Greek and mean "together." You can remember *syn-* easily by thinking of "synonym." A synonym is a word that goes "together" with another word because it has a similar meaning.

You can remember *sym-* by thinking of "symphony," which is a group of instruments making sound "together." The whole is more than the sum of its parts.

As we *syn*thesize what is known about these prefixes, we become *sym*pathetic towards them. Think with me about these terms:

- *syn*onym: a word that can be placed "together" with another due to closeness in meaning
- *syn*tax: an arranging "together" of words in a sentence to make it meaningful
- *syn*chronize: to place two clocks "together" in keeping time
- *syn*agogue: a place where people are led "together" in worship
- *syn*thesis: a placing "together" of separate elements into a unified whole
- *sym*phony: a sounding "together" of instruments
- *sym*metry: two objects that can be measured "together" perfectly
- *sym*bol: a sign put "together" with that which it represents
- *syn*ergy: energy created "together" with another

We often say that we can do more together than we could ever do by ourselves. That's synergy. Synergy is a powerful force to be released once it has been harnessed. When two people possess synergy, they work well together and create a positive, flowing energy that has multiplying impact. As networkers our focus is not so much on unity as it is on harmony. Synergistically speaking, all of us have a note to sing in the same song, a skill to offer in the same project.

Let's think about this carefully. When we have all the parts to something, how is that different from the whole thing? What needs to be added to make a whole? The answer is relationship and connection. The parts of a bicycle spread out on the garage floor are not a bicycle. Only the pieces assembled—that is, arranged and connected in proper relationship—are a bicycle.

Note that such special relationships and connections, chosen out of hundreds of possible relationships and connections, generate something "more" for the parts and for the whole. In the case of the bicycle, the pedals have to be in a special relationship with the wheels to enable the rider's feet to propel the bicycle forward. If the pedals are where the seat should be, they can't do their job. That "right relationship" is synergy.

In a living system, another word for this is "health." To the extent that all the parts of a living system are in right relationship to each other and to the system as a whole, that system is healthy. Linguistically, the word "health" derives from the same root as the word "whole," as in "wholesome." Right relationship, synergy, connectedness, and health are all aspects of the power that makes the whole more than the sum of its parts.

There are two kinds of synergy: static and dynamic. In static synergy, the power derives simply from the design—the way things are placed in relation to each other—such as in a beautiful flower arrangement. For example, there is static synergy in the strength of a triangle. Metal beams holding up a bridge or a geodesic dome have more strength because they're arranged as triangles rather than squares. The triangle shape itself, which is pure relationship, has intrinsic strength independent of the strength of the beams. The poles in a geodesic dome provide more strength collectively than they do individually, simply because they are arranged in triangles. The poles aren't doing anything. They're just sitting there in triangles being strong.

Dynamic synergy, in contrast, involves interactions that create, generate, or enable something. In dynamic synergy the power of the relationship derives from the active interaction of the people or things involved, as with a trio of jazz musicians in "a groove." Interestingly, diversity is a prerequisite for truly dynamic synergy. If everyone in a conversation has the same perspective, the result will be low-level synergy at best. It will certainly be nothing particularly exciting or productive. However, if many diverse views are allowed to surface through good communication processes, then those differences will almost certainly stimulate a blossoming of new and creative ideas that no one had considered before the conversation began. The whole can become greater than the sum of its parts to the extent that those parts are different and those differences are handled creatively.

New levels of organization and phenomena can only emerge from new combinations of things different in form, function, perspective, and so on. With learning and dialogue, ideas, perspectives, and experiences can mix and match, stimulating the creative birth and death of new ideas, perspectives, and experiences into a world of greater understanding. This is dynamic synergy.

Static and dynamic synergy both have to do with the relationship between parts. But, there is another major category of synergistic relationship that makes a whole greater than the sum of its parts: the relationship of the parts to the whole itself.

In a bicycle each part has a function that derives from, and contributes to, the function of the entire bicycle. There are wheels for moving, handlebars for steering, and pedals for setting everything in motion. All contribute to getting the biker to where he or she is going. Similarly, each organ of the body has a very specific relationship to the function of the whole body. Each plant and animal species has a specific relationship to the function of an entire ecosystem. The whole is greater than the sum of its parts, not only because there is synergy between the parts, but because the parts contribute to the whole and manifest its essence, purpose, or function.

The relationship goes both ways. The whole has a special relationship to its parts. At the most basic level, the whole is the reason for the part's existence. The logic of the whole governs the life of the part. The wheel by itself has little logic to its presence without being part of the bicycle. Its purpose is tied to the larger purpose of mobility.

A whole, healthy organization or community cares for its members. Any whole needs parts that are in good condition in order to function well, so it behooves the whole to care for its parts. Often benefits occur at every level. For example, when a group of people together articulate a common vision, that vision

(a) gives meaning to their individual lives, (b) coordinates their individual actions, sometimes with little explicit direction, (c) simplifies their interactions with each other and with group-level functionaries, (d) inspires mutual aid among comrades, and (e) increases the strength and coherence of the group as a whole—all at once!

As networkers we can use synergy with our Lord to enhance our synergy with each other and the world. A team can work really well together and generate a lot of *internal* synergy. But, when that team "gets in the flow" of a greater purpose, it joins a larger energy that makes everything seem effortless. When we as Christians leaders choose to pray together, we synergize together to seek the Lord and His will for our lives and ministries. When we take the next step and choose as a group of leaders to become more synergized together with God, we become more than just a group. We become a net that works! The greater "more-ness" that we experience is in addition to the "more-ness" that we already have through the synergy of our relationships with one another and with the group as a whole. We are more than the sum of our parts. We are even more than the whole. We are a synergistic network that is capable of achieving outcomes that are exponentially more than we could ever achieve as individuals.

The Mending of the Net

Synergy is not something that we can take for granted. Sometimes networks start off strong but grow weak because we fail to maintain them. It is far easier to keep a net strong by giving it regular attention than it is to have to go back and repair it due to neglect. As we endeavor to build a net that works, we need to make an effort to mend our nets each week. Just as the early disciples mended their nets after each use, so should we. How do we go about mending the net?

First, we should *attend* to the net. It is your responsibility, not someone else's. Since the network is made up of people, there needs to be consistent contact. Synergy requires the maintenance of good relationships. Develop a strategic plan of communication and stay faithful to it.

Second, we should *assess* the net. Think through the strengths and weaknesses of your network. If there has been some tearing of the relationship between you and someone else or between fellow networkers, it is far better to know about it sooner rather than later.

It is far easier to keep a net strong by giving it regular attention than it is to have to go back and repair it due to neglect.

Third, we should *address* the net. When a knot is unraveling or a string of communication is breaking, address it biblically, practically, socially, and strategically. Since the Billion Soul Network's rule book is the Bible, we always begin with biblical applications. The Bible is our relational road map. Once we have addressed the problem biblically, the additional layers of needed work usually become obvious to us.

If something practical is out of sync, fix it. If there is a deep hurt, get on a plane if necessary and go resolve it! If other people need to be included in the mending process, seek them out socially and bring them in. If the people around you have allowed little things to frustrate them, remind them what the mission is and get them focused again on the big picture. Nothing kills synergy quicker than losing sight of the greater goal.

Networking Is Broadened When We Shift Our World View

So far we have discussed the first and second levels of correct thinking that we, as networking leaders, must teach our inner circle in order to create a movement that moves and a network that works. The third level is this: *Networking is broadened when we shift our worldview.* Not only do we need to teach the right purpose and the right process, we must also teach the right paradigms.

The Right Paradigms

It was the mid-1990s when I heard the word *paradigm* for the very first time. I was attending the Evangelical Divinity School in Deerfield, Illinois, and I watched a film presentation that highlighted the topic of paradigms. Shortly thereafter, I rented that film for several hundred dollars so that I could show it to scores of other evangelists at the Assembly of God World Headquarters. I wanted these ministers to understand that the way they see their world has a great impact on the way they minister.

A paradigm is a pattern. It is the grid by which we view the world. If our worldview is narrow or out-of-date, then our ministry will be narrow and out-of-date too. The Church today needs more than leadership; we need "leader-shift." Significant paradigm shifts are impacting our world today. We either shift with them or we will become ineffective. It's like a parade that is passing by; we can choose to be bystanders and wave from the sidelines or we can choose to join in and become marchers ourselves.

I'm not saying that we should change everything that we think and do because the world is changing. But there are some paradigm shifts that are worth taking. In the years to come, we would be wise to make a least seven key paradigm shifts:

1. A power shift from self to God.

It saddens me that I have to bring this up in a book written for a Christian leadership audience. The truth of the matter is that many of God's people, especially in the West, have become selfish and self-centered. If we're going to build a thriving global network, we cannot do it from a position of selfishness. An effective leadership network cannot be built on our own personal foundation. It can only be built on the foundation of the King of the universe. In all of our planning, philosophizing, studying, creating, and networking, we must think beyond ourselves. We must think beyond our lifetime. We must think about the next generation and even on into eternity. We must make the power shift from self to God.

2. A priority shift from in-reach to outreach.

Most churches in the United States are not seeing salvation growth. They may be seeing transfer growth, but they're not seeing new people come to Christ. In fact, the "growth" in over 95 percent of the churches in the West is simply Christians moving from one church to another.

We need to get outward-focused. If we get wrapped up in the people we're not keeping rather than the people we're not reaching, then our past is the best we're going to be. We need to be more concerned for the lost, the people we're not reaching, than the people that may be moving from one church to another. We need a priority shift. We need to make the fundamental decision that we're going to put Jesus Christ back in our worship services and include regular invitations for people to come to Him as their Savior.

3. A programmatic shift from events to relationships.

The Billion Soul Network conducts a number of events every year in the United States and around the world. We actually go around the globe every three years with Billion Soul Summits held in various world regions. A summit is not held just to have an event; it is held as an opportunity for synergistic relationships to come together. When we have our biannual Synergize Conference in Orlando, Florida, with leaders from around the world, it is not about registration. It is about relationship. It is not about the event itself. It is about equipping the right people and connecting key individuals together. It is about tying knots to help build and broaden a net that works.

As networkers, we need to get to the point that we're not putting a date on the calendar just so we can attend another conference. Rather, we're choosing to connect with people, to tie knots, at a certain place and time. It's a programmatic shift in our thinking, moving from events to relationships.

4. A people shift from ministers to equippers.

We also need to see ourselves more as equippers than ministers. If sermons were going to save the world, we'd have saved the world a long time ago. Please don't misunderstand. We need the sermon, we need the sermonizer, we need the preacher, and we need the text from which we proclaim the Word. Sermons alone aren't going to get the job done, however. We must move from being only ministers to equippers, from adders to multipliers, and from preachers to teachers.

5. A provision shift from consumers to contributors.

For too long we in the Church have had a consumer mentality. We've focused on what we can get rather than what we can give. As networkers, we need to be contributors, not consumers. All of us have much to contribute to the global Church and to the fulfillment of the Great Commission. Today's technology makes it possible for every church to be a satellite church, for every pastor to help proliferate the gospel throughout the four corners of the world. In the past, it was the West going to the rest. Today it is the best around the world going to the rest. It is the global Church going to the global Church. All of this represents a major provision shift.

6. A perspective shift from church to Kingdom.

How do you view your ministry? How do you view your work? Do you see yourself working for the King of the universe or do you see yourself working for your denomination, your congregation, or your board of deacons? We need to move from a church-based mentality to a Kingdom mentality. As I have traveled throughout the world, it has become obvious to me that the churches the Lord is truly blessing today are Kingdom-minded, Great Commission churches. These are the churches that are very intentional in establishing the Kingdom of God in places where it has never been established before.

7. A process shift from older to younger.

Every once in a while I'm asked, "Which do you like better, the ocean or the mountains?" I love the mountains and I have been fortunate to see some of the great mountain ranges of the world. But if I had to choose, I would choose the ocean every time. I love walking along the beach and watching the waves. There are always two waves in motion: one that is going out, and one that is coming in. Without exception, the wave that is going out is always overtaken by the one that is coming in.

Whether we like it or not, the day will come when someone new will sit where we sit, lead where we lead and preach where we preach. The day will come when you and I will not be here. There is a great global shift underway. One generation is graduating for glory as another generation is coming in to take its place.

I am not worried about the future of the Church. I believe the next generation is going to go further and do more to expand the Kingdom of God than the current generation. I'm more concerned about leaders not being willing to allow the inevitable to happen. It is one thing to make a place for the youth that God is raising up. It is another thing to be willing to permit them take our place. It's time for all of us to get in line with what God is doing. He is raising up a young, vibrant global Church that one day will take our place. That is not negative. That is positive. It is a process shift from the older to the younger that will bring great glory to God.

As you think about developing and deploying a global network that works, consider what you need to do to equip your inner circle of leadership relationships. Consider how you can help the men and women God has put into your life to move forward with the right purpose, the right process, and the right paradigms. As you equip your inner circle, not only will each individual become stronger, but relationships will deepen, synergy will flow, and your network will impact the world in greater ways than you ever imagined.

8

Encourage Your Confidence

All of us need encouraging words and encouraging people in our lives if we are to fulfill our divine destiny in our lifespan. When I think about great leaders of the past and great contemporaries of the present, I realize that all of them, without exception, had to fight the good fight of faith. They had to see through what they started, and along the way, they needed encouragement to keep them keeping on. The Bible is clear, from the early history of the Book of Genesis to the late words of the Apostle John on the Isle of Patmos, that we all need times of refreshment, renewal, and resources to keep going until our job is completed.

The truth is that networking is hard work. Sometimes we're so excited about the "net" that we underestimate the "work" involved in developing and deploying it. It is one thing for us to get people together; it is quite another thing to mobilize great people for a cause and in a direction that produces effective synergy and results in a phenomenal outcome that could never be achieved by individuals alone.

And yet, at times, people can speak such discouraging words to us that we want to give up before we even get started! So, let me begin with these words of encouragement: After ten years of birthing, building, and broadening a global network, I can honestly tell you that the pleasure has been worth the pain and the privilege of connecting relationally with some of the finest brothers and sisters in the Body of Christ has been worth the price.

God's Five Keys of Encouragement

In Chapter 1 we introduced the story of Eliazar, the servant of Abraham who was given the task of finding a wife for Isaac. Like all of us, Eliazar needed encouragement to complete his assignment. In fact, the encouragement that Eliazar received to make him prosperous on his path and give him God's speed on his way can be summed up in five phrases that hold the keys to our encouragement as well.

1. The Right Promise

Before Eliazar began his journey, Abraham told him, "[God] will send His angel before you" (Gen. 24:7). I like that promise! Our Lord dispatches His angels ahead of us to help us to be successful. God Himself gave His promise through Abraham to Eliazar that He would lead, direct, and protect him. He would put the right people in his path to help him, encourage him, and make him successful. I believe that for all of us, there are more promises than there are problems. God's promises renew us and help us to finish what we begin. The fulfillment of the Great Commission isn't my idea or yours; it's God's, and the promise of God is in the midst of it.

2. The Right Prayer

Eliazar was a prayerful servant. When you look at how he went about his business, you see that he prayed his way to victory. In the city of Nahor, he prayed, "O Lord, the God of my master Abraham, grant me success today" (Gen. 24:12). God answered by directing him how to identify Rebekah at a spring where women came to draw water.

If you are not praying, one of two things is true. Either you believe that your assignment is not God-given, or you are overly confident and don't think you need God's direction. In fact, as networkers, you and I need God's favor in everything that we do. That favor comes through our prayer time before the Lord.

3. The Right People

Without spending time with the right people in the right places, you will never become the right person. I have repeated this phrase more than once in this book because I'm convinced it's a bedrock principle for becoming the people God intends us to be.

Certainly, we get encouragement directly from God and His Word, but we also get it from His people. Hebrews 12:1 says, "Since we have a great cloud of witnesses surrounding us . . . let us run with endurance the race that is set before us." The people who make up that "great cloud of witnesses" are listed in Hebrews 11. What are they there for? They're there to encourage us, cheer us on, inspire us to run the race and be about the business of the Master.

Without spending time with the right people in the right places, you will never become the right person.

People either encourage us or they discourage us. They either make withdrawals or they make deposits. They either brighten our lives or they dim them. It's important that we network with the right people. Sometimes beginning networkers make the mistake of believing that all they need to do is get some people together and a network is born. I have learned from experience that it is far better to go a little slower and get the *right* people together than to end up with one or two people who have hidden agendas, who will in time disrupt, dismantle, or destroy the network that God wants you to build.

4. The Right Process

In the last chapter we talked about developing the right process, because the right process produces the right product and the right outcomes; wrong process, wrong product. It is important that we develop processes in our lives that make life simpler and help to speed us on our way to do what God has called us to do. Our value will be measured by what we produce for others. We will be rewarded according to this value.

5. The Right Profit

When things get tough, thinking about the right profit, the bottom line, and the ultimate outcome can definitely encourage us. What will be the result when we are successful and an effective network is built and broadened? Will it be churches planted, souls saved, or unreached people groups adopted? Focusing on these outcomes will renew our minds and encourage us to push through difficulties in order to complete God's assignment.

God's Three Principles of Empowerment

Eliazar's mission to find a wife for Isaac was successful. He crossed the finish line. Many years later, Joseph, Isaac's grandson, was getting ready to cross a finish line of his own. The familiar story can be found in the last chapter of the Book of Genesis. Just before his death, Joseph pulled his family together and recommitted them to the mission that was before them. He reminded them of where they were going. He understood how important it was for those who came after him to continue pursuing God's vision. Then, he released himself to be with the Lord.

Hebrews 11:22 recaps it this way, "Joseph, when he was dying, made mention of the exodus of the sons of Israel, and gave orders concerning his bones." What's amazing about this story is that 25 percent of the Book of Genesis is devoted to this one person named Joseph, and yet Hebrews 11, the Great Hall of Fame of Faith chapter, gives him only one verse. When Joseph "made mention of the exodus . . . and gave orders concerning his bones," God smiled upon the entirety of his life because of the faith demonstrated in this last act.

You and I can draw great encouragement from Joseph's story. Remembering three principles that Joseph learned over his lifetime can greatly assist us in fulfilling everything the Lord has called us to be and do in this life. These principles can help us get to where He has called us to go.

1. The Unbreakable Promises of God

First of all, we need to remember the unbreakable promises of God. Hundreds of years before this scene from Joseph's life, the Lord gave promises to Joseph's great-grandfather, Abraham, about his lineage. God told Abraham that he would have a son in his old age. This son would become a great nation, the nation would eventually be relocated in a distant land, they would be forced into slavery, there would be a miraculous exodus, and finally, the people would come back to the land of Canaan. The process, God said, would take at least four hundred years.

Essentially, here's what the Lord was telling Abraham, "Abraham, I'm making a promise to you. The promise is larger than you are and it's longer than your life span. By the time this promise is fulfilled, you will be at peace with your fathers."

Abraham believed God's promise, so he sent Eliazar to seek out a bride for Isaac. Rebekah was found and the process began for the nation of Israel to be born and to broaden throughout the earth.

Joseph never forgot the unbreakable promise that God had given to his ancestors. We know from Genesis that Joseph's life was often difficult. No doubt there were times when he was discouraged and felt defeated by his circumstances. Yet, he did not let the dream die. Joseph did not let the promise be taken from him. He understood what the promise was and he understood what the plan was. Regardless of the pit, the prison, the palace, or the pharaoh, Joseph remained faithful to his assignment.

You and I need to remember the unbreakable promises of God. There are times when the problems and stress and difficulties of life can discourage the best of us. As I've said before, there are more promises than there are problems. The Holy Trinity never meets in an emergency session. God is not worried about providing for you or for me.

Many leaders say, "I wish I had enough money to pursue my dream." Most of the time we don't have a money problem. We have a vision problem. If you don't have a vision, it doesn't take much money to fund that. However, if you have a God-sized vision, you need a God-sized provision to fulfill it. The question isn't "Do I have enough money?" It's "Do I have enough vision?" Out of the vision comes the provision.

When Joseph was in the land of Egypt, he wasn't impressed with the pyramids. He wasn't impressed by the wealth of Pharaoh. He understood that God had him on a divine assignment. He saw his role in God's goal. He saw his part in God's heart and he was faithful to see it through. Joseph placed the vision in the hearts of his children and grandchildren so that they could continue the assignment long after he was gone

The original promise was spoken to Abraham. Joseph was one of those who understood it in his generation. Likewise, the promises of God were not first and foremost given to us; but, like Joseph, we have inherited them. Wise is the networking leader who gets in sync with where God is going and asks God to bless and to prosper his path. One day the glory of the Lord will cover the earth like the water covers the sea. There is not one dry spot on the bottom of the ocean, and one day there will not be a dry spot where the glory of the Lord has not kissed the earth. The Bible tells us in Revelation 7 that every tongue, tribe, and nation will one day stand before the throne of God. This is going to happen whether we get involved or not. The Lord will pass us by if we don't get in sync with His plan.

Some people try to break God's promises, and they end up being broken by them. We can either be blessed by God's promises or be broken by God's promises, but we will never bend the promises of God. Just as Joseph had to pull the right people together in his generation to achieve God's purpose, the Lord will empower us according to His promises.

2. The Unshakeable Power of God

Secondly, we need to realize the unshakeable power of God. Companies open and companies close. Denominations start up and denominations slow down. Empires are raised up and empires come crashing down. However, the Kingdom of God has never experienced a recession! The Kingdom of God is continuing to grow each year. In fact, the Church is growing faster today than it has ever grown before. We are living in the greatest time in world history for evangelism, church planting, and global networking. Because of the unshakeable power of God, it is entirely possible for the Great Commission to be fulfilled in this century.

Let's look again at what Joseph chose to do in Genesis 50, when he knew he was about to be with the Lord. No doubt there were concerns all around him. Joseph understood that life was about to change for him and for those following after him. How did Joseph handle the situation? When he pulled his family members together, did he fill them with worry, anxiety, dread, and doubt? No. He reminded them of God's plan. He reminded them of the mission and where they were headed. He reminded them that God was going to see the vision through to the end. He encouraged them by ensuring them that everything was going to work out wonderfully down the road because of the unbreakable promises and the unshakeable power of God.

The question isn't "Do I have enough money?"
It's "Do I have enough vision?" Out of the vision
comes the provision.

In fact, Joseph had demonstrated this understanding years earlier, when his father, Jacob, had passed away. Joseph was in the middle of an important assignment in Egypt and yet he stopped what he was doing and took his father's body back to Canaan, to the small village of Shechem, which means "a place of prosperity." He took his father back to prosperity, buried him there and then returned to Egypt, staying on the assignment. Joseph realized where his home would be and where his people were going, and so he made a deposit by burying his father in the Promised Land.

Would there be labor instead of favor in their future? Yes. Would there be famine instead of feasting? Yes. Would there be hardship, headache, and heartache? Yes. But God would see them through to the other side. Frankly, it doesn't matter who the pharaoh is or how many chariots you have. When God says he's going to do something, you can count on it. He's going to do it.

There were concerns all around Joseph. No doubt there are concerns all around you. There are financial and family concerns. There are health and ministerial concerns. You may be facing any number of difficult obstacles as you build your network. Let me assure you, the Lord wants to help you finish what you started. He wants to give you enough money, enough momentum, and enough people in your life to be able to achieve what you can only do by networking together.

Joseph not only faced concerns. He faced change. Real, dramatic changes were taking place. Likewise, radical change in the world is impacting your life and mine. This generation, especially in the last ten to fifteen years, has experienced more change than any other generation since the beginning of time. In the last twenty to thirty years, dramatic change in information technology has catapulted the nations of the earth forward in a way that no previous generation has ever experienced. Should we be fearful of this change? No, we should welcome it.

Joseph knew that change was coming. He knew that his time on the earth would soon be over. Not only did he understand what he had to do; he knew that he had to do it quickly and decisively so that his family members would be able to continue what he (and his ancestors) had started. Oftentimes when people reflect on their legacy, they think, "What am I leaving behind?" Personally, I don't think so much about what I'm leaving behind, but rather, "What have I started while here on the earth?" My prayer is that I start more ripples than I will ever be able to see to the end during this short tenure in the world.

It's important to understand the chronology that is behind us. We have come a long way in a short period of time. When I think about the birthing of the Billion Soul Network just at the beginning of this millennium and where it is today, I am amazed. BSN is a network that started with just two people and now encompasses more than 1,450 different denominations and organizations and more than 450,000 churches in ten short years! The history behind us is prologue and the future before us is bright because of the unshakeable power of God.

He is the "extra" that turns the ordinary into the extraordinary: the extra thoughts that He puts in our minds, the extra faith that He builds in our hearts, the extra abilities that He deposits in our lives, and the extra people that He sends along our path so that we can do the extraordinary and fulfill the Great Commission in our generation. It doesn't matter what else happens in the world in the years ahead. God is going to keep His word.

3. The Unmistakable Peace of God

Third, we need to rest in the unmistakable peace of God. Sometimes we wonder, "Is the Lord going to come through? Is He going to be on time?" The fact is the Lord is never late. He always comes through with His plan for His person.

Think of Joseph. As he was crossing the finish line, he smiled at Death. I'm sure you don't have anything worse than Death stalking you. I know I don't. Joseph was at peace as he smiled at Death and his family members lay him to rest. One year went by, five years went by, a hundred years went by, a total of four hundred years went by. Then one day Moses walked into Pharaoh's court and demanded, "Let my people go." That was the day of divine exodus that God had told Abraham about centuries earlier. It was one of the big, red-letter days on God's calendar. On that day, Moses, the great general, led nearly two million people out of Egypt toward the Promised Land.

Before they had gone very far, Moses gave the command, "Go and find the body of Joseph. Remember what our ancestors told us concerning his bones? We need to bury him in Canaan." Don't think for one second that Moses and the people left Joseph behind! I was taught in Sunday school that only two people who came out of Egypt—Caleb and Joshua—actually went into the Promised Land. In fact, there were three who entered the Promised Land. Joseph was the third.

I believe that as the people brought Joseph out of Egypt, they took him to the front of the line. Of course, the Bible doesn't tell us where they positioned Joseph's bones on the trip, but I have a hard time believing that they carried him behind two million people. I think it is more likely that they brought him to where Moses was, leading the pack. How long did they carry him? They carried him through the Red Sea. They carried him through the forty years of wilderness wanderings. They carried him by Mount Sinai. They carried him by Mount Nebo, where God buried Moses. But, Joseph didn't stop there; he continued right on. What is so amazing is that they buried Israelites every day in the wilderness; in fact, they buried an entire generation of Israelites, while God raised up a new generation to go into the Promised Land. But Joseph wasn't buried in the land of wilderness wanderings; he was taken all the way to Canaan. There was more faith in the bones of Joseph than there was in the feet of the Israelites. Joseph crossed the Jordan and went through Gilgal and Jericho. He was there the day the sun stood still.

How do I know this? The Bible tells me so. Joshua 24:22 says, "Now they buried the bones of Joseph, which the sons of Israel brought up from Egypt, at Shechem"—the place of prosperity where Joseph had buried his father, Jacob, more than one hundred years earlier.

You and I need to remember the unbreakable promises of God, move forward in the unshakeable power of God, and rest in the unmistakable peace of God.

What an amazing story! Joseph was sold into slavery, falsely accused, put into prison, brought to the palace, and made second in command in a nation that was not his own. He was buried in Egypt, carried through the wilderness wanderings, brought into the Promised Land, and finally buried next to his father in Shechem. What God begins, He finishes!

As we work to build a network to evangelize, to mobilize, and to synergize for Great Commission fulfillment, there will be problems; there will be demonic attacks; there will be financial challenges; there will be storms that will come our way. That's when you and I need to remember the unbreakable promises of God, move forward in the unshakeable power of God, and rest in the unmistakable peace of God. God will give us the encouragement to see our assignment through to the end.

There is no task more important. Throughout history there have been many people we might identify as "change agents" in the world. But how many of them could say at the end of life's journey, "Not only did I help to bring change, but I helped to bring salvation"?

As we close this chapter, I want to ask one final, perplexing question. Why didn't Joseph want his bones left in Egypt? Why didn't he simply encourage his family, "Go on to the land of Canaan and one day we will all rendezvous in glory"? Why was he so emphatic in his insistence, "When God takes you out, you must take me with you"? I believe the answer is simply this: Joseph wanted to be involved in what God was doing, whether he was dead or alive. He had an unquenchable desire to be included in God's plan to establish the Kingdom on the earth.

If you cultivate that kind of passion for God's vision, your reservoir will never run dry, and your fountainhead will never be dammed up. You will never burn out nor will you rust out. Instead, you will be encouraged and renewed in your mind, heart and soul by God Himself. *You* will be the change agent. *You* will be the one who brings salvation. And you will be the master networker who helps to fulfill the Great Commission in your lifetime and mine.

9

Exemplify Your Commitment

You've probably heard the phrase, "It's not what you know, it's who you know." In today's interconnected society that axiom rings true now more than ever. Our talents, our abilities and our experience will never take us anywhere if nobody knows we exist. In order to get where we want to go in life, in business and in ministry, we need to be resourceful, and our fellow human beings are our vast resource.

How do we connect with this resource? How do we present ourselves and our causes to people whose support and assistance would make all the difference in our ability to succeed? The key is to exemplify our commitment to the Lord, to our network, to our vision and to them as individuals and leaders. Here is another axiom I have used before: Just as we cannot teach what we do not know and cannot give what we do not have, we cannot lead others where we have not been. We need to demonstrate that we know where we are going and that we know how to lead others there too.

Eight Steps to Effective Networking

Unless you're an extroverted person who thoroughly enjoys getting out and about, networking with others can be exhausting. Connecting with the "vast resource" of potential relationships is not easy; it takes both time and effort. You may ask, "So why bother?" Imagine how much time and frustration you would save if anything you wanted or needed to move forward in ministry was just one or two phone calls away! Ultimately, a network can be an investment with benefits that outweigh the costs. You just need to stick with it and watch it grow. Here are eight steps that will help you get started and keep going.

1. Break your networking stereotypes.

Since you're reading this book, I assume you're familiar with the benefits of networking. Perhaps you have avoided doing it for any number of reasons. To some, networking can seem insincere or pretentious or even manipulative. If that's what you're thinking, then you're probably right in some cases. There will always be people who judge others based on image and title. There will always be those who take advantage and give little in return. There are also people who sincerely want to build networking relationships that are genuine and mutually beneficial. As you network, you're going to have to sift through the people you *don't* want to know in order to get to the people that you *do* want to know.

As you network, you're going to have to sift through the people you don't want to know in order to get to the people that you do want to know.

The good news is that with practice, you'll get better and better at spotting people worth knowing. You might think you're too shy or self-conscious to converse with certain leaders. Networking does require a degree of boldness, getting out of your shell, and stepping out of the box. Even shy people tend to be more open and talkative when they're doing and talking about something that deeply interests them. Besides, with the advent of Internet social networking sites, you can find others with similar interests and goals without being in a room full of people. Once you find people who are just as passionate about a subject as you are, then networking becomes much easier. It always helps to be approachable. Over time it will get easier for you to start a conversation with a complete stranger.

2. Build your social network.

If you hate small talk, this may be one of the hardest parts of networking for you. I promise you will improve with practice. The key is to take genuine interest in other people's lives. A good stepping stone is to begin strengthening your existing connections. Get in touch with old friends, distant relatives, and people you went to school with. You'll be reaching out but you won't be approaching strangers. Make a phone call or send an e-mail to find out where they are and what they're doing, and make sure to tell them what you're involved with in life.

Another stepping stone is to pursue interests and activities that mean a lot to you. The Internet has made this a lot easier. Check out forums, listings, classifieds, internet mailings, or listserves for meetings and events that are likely to attract people with similar interests and passions. Go to work or ministry-related conferences. Make contacts with politicians and their aides by getting involved with their political party or volunteering in an election. Whatever the meeting, print out business cards and give them out to the people you connect with. Ask them for their business cards and write any details you want to remember about them on the backs of the cards.

Start small. Don't sign up to go to twelve meetings in one month. Keeping up a sustained effort over the long run is better than making a one-time big push and then burning out or not keeping your promises. Remember that networking requires maintenance. You don't want to bite off more than you can chew.

3. Find out who knows whom.

When you're talking to people, find out what they do for a living and for fun. Find out what their spouse, family members, or close friends do for work and recreation. It may be helpful to make note of this in your address book or on a notepad in your smartphone so you don't lose track of who does what.

Find the extroverts, especially if you tend to be more introverted. As you continue to network, you will find that some people are much better at it than you are. They already know everyone. Get to know *them*. In turn, they can introduce you to others who share your interests or goals.

4. Find ways to spend time with people.

A great way to begin building a networking relationship is to invite someone you've met to go out for lunch or coffee or do something related to a common interest. If you meet someone at a friend's gathering, for example, and you think you have mutual interests or goals, find a way to spend more time with that individual, preferably one-on-one. The objective is to establish a connection beyond your initial meeting.

5. Be generous.

Since your goal is to develop mutually beneficial relationships, a good kick-start is to find ways to help others. I'm not necessarily talking about contacts, job referrals, or loans. A compliment, a listening ear, and other less tangible gestures of kindness and generosity can be just as significant. The key is to be sincere as you work to establish good relations with others and open channels for mutual benefit.

I do have one word of caution, however. Watch out for parasites, people who try to pump you for favors but never want to help you in return. When you find a parasite attached to you, turn them down as politely as you can. "No, I'm sorry, I cannot do that tomorrow. I've got plans." If they try to make you feel guilty for not responding the way they want you to, find a way to get out of the conversation and then make yourself scarce. Don't be cold or lose your temper. That will give them something negative to say about you when they're talking to others. "Oh, yes, I know so and so. He once called me a leech." I'm talking from experience. Don't let this happen to you!

6. Follow up.

Don't get someone's business card or e-mail address and forget about it. Find a way to stay in touch. Maintain your network. If you run across an article that may be of interest to someone, send it to them. If you know of a negative event like a tornado or electrical blackout that has happened in their vicinity, call them to make sure they're okay. Keep track of birthdays and mark them on a calendar. Send birthday cards along with friendly notes to let them know you haven't forgotten about them. They won't forget about you either.

7. Tap into your network.

The next time you need something such as a job, an employee, a partner in launching a venture, or some other resource, cast a wide net and see what happens. Make a few phone calls or send out e-mails describing your situation in a friendly tone, "Hey, I'm in a bit of a pinch. I have this situation that's come up and I really need your assistance." Don't ever apologize when asking for help or a favor. It signals a lack of confidence and professionalism. There's nothing to be sorry about. You're just seeing if anyone is in a position to be able to help you. You're not making demands or forcing people to do something they don't want to do.

8. Use the Internet.

We've already mentioned the Internet more than once. It's a very useful tool for meeting and keeping in contact with a very large amount of people worldwide. Let's face it, not all of us are living in cities like New York or Los Angeles where it's relatively easy to find someone with a mutual interest and to get in touch with them personally. Social networking has evolved over recent years to become a business and ministry networking tool as well. Online networking through the Internet has effectively reduced the distance between any two people to zero. You can network not only with people in your hometown, but also with people in other cities and other states, from coast to coast and around the world.

Make an effort to develop some online networking contacts. Search for journals and professional organizations online and use resources that are available on the Internet to help you connect further with more people. In fact, use every online tool at your disposal to build a social network in real life. Instant message applications, for instance, are sometimes better than phone calls.

Networking with Busy People

The networking steps I've just described are effective for beginning and maintaining a growing network. I want to go one step further. You see, many of the key people you will want to meet and network with, the ones who may be in the best position to significantly broaden and strengthen your network and help you achieve your goals, are very busy. They're leaders of churches, businesses, organizations, or denominations. Their support and advice is sought after. Sometimes their names are quite well known. The question is, how do you network with them? How do you network with leaders whose time is so very limited? It's one thing to network with peers and colleagues who you connect with casually or who God puts in your path providentially. It's another thing to network with the leaders, the mentors, the "mountains of ministry," and the master networkers you want to meet but whose friendship and support may seem beyond your reach.

Busy people can be very valuable contacts for you and your network. They're busy for a reason! But more often than not, the people you will most want to network with are the least accessible. Busy leaders are bombarded with endless e-mails, phone calls, social media connections, and much, much more. Making contact with them is difficult because so many others are trying to do the same thing. Does that mean you can't be successful? Not at all.

I believe I can share some solid, practical advice on reaching busy people for two reasons. First, I've been fortunate to network with scores of busy people during my fifteen to twenty years of networking experience. I've had to learn what works and what doesn't work in the real world. Second, I know how busy people tend to filter and process their communications, because I am a busy person who processes a lot of communication. I have received tens of thousands of e-mails over the years. I don't have the capacity to accept deeper connections with everyone who wants to build a bridge with me, so I have to be selective.

I handle new communication requests in the same way that many other busy people do. Most of my decisions are based on common sense and necessity. When would-be networkers overlook or ignore these simple realities, they pay the price for it. Some leaders choose to separate "business contacts" and "personal friends." For me, though, there isn't much distinction, since I've chosen to work in a networking ministry that believes all God's people are called to fulfill the Great Commission. All believers are called to network with one another at some level to achieve this great goal. It is a goal that can only be reached by all of us collectively working together.

You *can* make contact with busy people. From my experience on both sides of the equation, I offer these thirteen keys:

1. Understand the busy person's perspective.

You may think you have a very good reason for contacting a particular leader. You may have the noblest of intentions. However, if you don't look at it from the busy person's perspective, you may make a mistake that will result in the exact opposite of what you want.

Accept up front that a busy leader cannot or will not give you a serious slice of their time and attention without a good reason. The mere fact that you contacted them is not reason enough to expect a reply. Don't presume that you will get a response because you have an "intuitive feeling" that the two of you are supposed to connect. Busy people receive dozens and sometimes hundreds of incoming communications 365 days a year. They don't have the capacity to treat every request with equal importance. This usually means they will spend very little time processing communication with people they don't know or people they don't think will add value to their personal or global mission in life.

Busy people are often criticized for seeming to be unresponsive to reasonable requests. I used to think that such behavior was rude or unkind when I was subjected to it. My thinking changed when I was put in a position to experience it from the other side. I realized that I was spending hours answering e-mails and reading other people's comments, with little to show for it in terms of inner fulfillment or outer results. I knew then that I had to be more selective.

Busy people aren't trying to be rude. They're simply trying to be efficient and effective with what God has given them. Would you willingly volunteer to spend an extra hour per day answering e-mails every day for the rest of your life with no end in sight, if it weren't absolutely necessary? The answer is no.

Accept up front that a busy leader cannot or will not give you a serious slice of their time and attention without a good reason. The mere fact that you contacted them is not reason enough to expect a reply.

To effectively network with busy, sought-after people, you must accept and embrace the busy person's reality, rather than getting stuck in your own perspective and failing to empathize. Eventually, as your own network grows, you, too, will have to choose to be focused, so you can find the right people. I'm convinced the focus brings us to that reality.

2. Don't trigger a typical pattern.

In other words, don't send a busy person a communication that easily blends in with all the others they see every week. If your message doesn't stand out, it will most likely be processed as routine and unimportant. To your mind, of course, your message is important. You want to connect and network with this person to achieve something you feel passionate about. Your purpose in reaching out is genuine and heartfelt. But in all likelihood, your message isn't being received the way you intend it to be received. Make sure that when you're reaching out to a busy leader for the first time, you don't come across like everybody else with a message they've seen many, many times before.

3. Avoid making threats.

An example of a threat might be, "I really need a response from you, so I'm going to keep e-mailing you every day until you reply." In my experience, most people have the good sense not to use threats, but it does happen often enough that I can call it out as a pattern. Threats are almost always counterproductive. If you behave with such gross immaturity, you're simply going to paint yourself to busy leaders as someone they do *not* want to get to know, much less network with. It is never to your strategic advantage to make threats.

4. Bypass clogged channels.

For busy people, some communication channels are more clogged than others. If you try to get into a leader's life through the busier channels, you're just jumping into the slush pile along with everyone else. For example, if a busy leader has a strong online presence, it's a safe bet that e-mail is an extremely clogged channel. That's probably true for most busy people these days. If you want to drop someone a casual note and don't need a response, feel free to use e-mail. But if you want to establish first contact with a key leader for networking purposes, e-mail is probably the worst way to do it.

Generally speaking, if you use a generic communication medium to make contact, your message has a much higher chance of being regarded as generic and unimportant. Most online communication channels are very clogged, including e-mail, forums, Facebook, and Twitter. You will not have a good chance of building anything more than a casual connection through such channels.

Instead of e-mail, use channels that are not so clogged. Pick up the phone. Send a gift. FedEx a book with a letter. Better yet, go out of your way to meet the leader in person. I rarely try to make my first contact with someone through e-mail or the telephone. My personal preference is to make first contact face-to-face. Another good option is to ask a mutual friend to make an introduction. Once you make a lot of friends and contacts in a particular field, it's usually not hard to find someone who already knows the person you want to network with. I'll talk more about this shortly.

5. Avoid cold calling.

What do I mean by cold calling? I'm talking about blasting the same email message to large numbers of people in an untargeted or semi-targeted fashion. I'm not talking about sending a very targeted e-mail to specific people. Busy people get many "cold calls" or "cold e-mails" every day. This is yet another pattern that gets filtered. A cold call is essentially the same as email spam. And, as with spam, a cold call will sometimes result in a hit. However, for each hit you generate, you've pestered and annoyed a lot of other people. It's a very inefficient-form of networking.

The main reason cold calling is so popular is because it's brainless. It's easy, convenient, and takes little creative thought. It may take some courage to contact large numbers of people you don't know, and there is clearly a skill-set that can be developed for this. People have written whole books about it. But the main reason I believe good networkers should reject this approach is that it's a desperate move. There are far more intelligent and efficient means for reaching people than spamming them. Remember, we're striving to network with people. When someone sends me a spam-like message more than once, I simply set up a filter so that I don't see anything again from that source. This saves me a lot of time in the long run.

The face to face equivalent of cold calling is going around handing out business cards to every leader you meet. Earlier in this chapter, I suggested handing out business cards as a way to begin making social connections. Eventually, though, you will want to put the cards away. They're not a good method for making higher-level networking contacts. Frankly, I don't carry business cards and I haven't done so in twenty years.

Another problem with cold calling is that when you do get a lead, it's usually not a very good one. Deals that arise out of cold calling often take a significant amount of messaging to make them work. You end up with lots of mismatches, partial matches, and near-misses, which means more work and more stress in the long run. Busy people are often on the lookout for golden opportunities. The hit ratio from cold calling is simply so low that most leaders feel confident discarding communication that comes via this method.

6. Ask for an introduction.

If you want to connect with a busy or renowned leader, try to introduce yourself, if possible. Or, use the approach I alluded to earlier. Find an existing friend or contact who knows the person you want to meet and have that contact introduce you. This immediately elevates your status in the eyes of the leader and makes it easier for the leader to lower his or her shield. I have many friends and contacts that I trust to introduce me to other people, whether by phone, e-mail, or in person. The hit ratio of good connections that come to me through introductions from my existing network is significantly higher than I'd ever see from incoming cold calls. With cold calling, the ratio may be one good connection in 500, but with intros from my friends, the ratio is probably closer to one in three.

Of course, every friend or contact is different. Some contacts are higher-quality leads than others. I always pay attention to leads that come through my long-term friends and business associates, especially those that know me well. They understand what kinds of friends and contacts will be a good match or a good investment for me.

If you expect others to make introductions for you, you should be willing to do the same for them. Keep in mind, though, that some intros can be tricky. When friends are involved, I'm clear up front that I will do an intro only when I think it will potentially lead to a win-win relationship for everyone involved. I'm quite selective. Before taking action, I carefully consider what consequences would likely result from a particular introduction. If the consequences look good for everyone, I make the intro. If not, I pass. Usually, when the consequences don't look good, it's because the introduction would be lopsided. In that case, one person would simply suck ideas and energy from the other without offering any positive ideas or contacts in return.

7. Use a back door.

Busy leaders often have a back-door channel. When communication comes through this channel, they pay more attention to it. In order to use such channels effectively, it helps to have a genuine shared interest that is somewhat uncommon. For example, an excellent back door is whatever new interest the busy leader is just getting into. The door is wide open, because the leader doesn't know many people who share that interest yet. He or she is often eager to learn, share, and grow and is happy to connect on that basis. That's why it is so important to find out what people are interested in as we strive to get to know them.

8. Understand the problem of boredom.

Busy, well-known, and sought-after leaders want to avoid being swamped, overwhelmed, and bored to tears with "more of the same." Getting the same kind of communiques day in and day out can get dull fast. This is a really crucial point. Does it make sense to you? If you can understand and accept this part of the daily life of a busy person, you're probably in the top five percent of networkers—maybe in the top one percent.

Busy people still want to meet new people. They really do. They still want to connect, network, hang out, and have fun. They're not cold and rude. They need their social lives to be varied and interesting and by shielding themselves from mindless repetition, they're able to be more present when they do reach out and connect.

Personally, I enjoy connecting with people. I enjoy networking. I enjoy networking for greater, higher, and wiser goals for the Body of Christ. I'm not interested in getting together just to say I got together. I want my getting together with other key people to really count for the cause of Jesus Christ.

9. Don't apologize for reaching out.

Earlier I mentioned that you shouldn't apologize for tapping into your network. Neither should you apologize for reaching out to a busy leader.

Never begin your first contact with an apology. When people start notes to me with, "Sorry to bother you, but . . .," that tells me a great deal about their expectations for connecting with me. It says that they expect to be a bother.

If you hint that you're about to irritate or annoy someone, he or she will assume you're right. You may think you're being polite and respectful. Perhaps it would be more accurate to say that down deep inside you don't feel equal to the person you're contacting. If you feel that you have to apologize for bothering someone, maybe you shouldn't make the contact until you work a bit more on your self-esteem.

The most certain way to have your communication devalued is to signal upfront that you consider yourself a low-value contact. High-value contacts don't apologize for reaching out.

If you believe you should network with a particular person, approach the contact with confidence and strength and you are sure to get a better response. The most certain way to have your communication devalued is to signal upfront that you consider yourself a low-value contact. High-value contacts don't apologize for reaching out.

10. Get to the point.

When you communicate with a busy person, do your best to be clear, concise, and get to the point. Plainly state the purpose of the communication in your first sentence. Get to the franking point as quickly as possible and let the other person know the context of the rest of your message.

Never begin an e-mail (or letter or phone call) like this, "I know you get a lot of e-mails, but I just had to send you this message. I'm sure you must be very busy and I definitely respect your time, so I'll try to be as brief as possible. This request will take a bit of explaining, though, so please take the time to read it all the way through. I'm sure it will be worth your time." That is exactly the moment the busy person will hit "delete"! Whenever

I see such a paragraph, I usually think, "You don't have to apologize. You don't have to feel uncomfortable. Let's just get to the bottom line and find out if we can network together for a greater cause."

You may think that you should include as much detail as possible in your first message so that the busy leader will have all the important information he or she needs up front. After all, you've only got one shot at making a first impression, so the more words you use the better, right? That's a big mistake! Don't send a wall of text. More than two paragraphs is more than enough. If the point of your communication is to make a request or an offer, don't pretend that you're connecting on the basis of friendship. That's inauthentic. You're better off cutting out the fluff and keeping your message short and sweet. Show the value of your proposal. What's in it for the leader? How can the two of you achieve something that neither one of you could do by yourself?

11. Keep your personality switched on.

The way that you normally behave with your friends and family is how you should behave when connecting with busy people, renowned leaders, and those you look to for mentoring. Be yourself. I've seen people act like deer caught in headlights when meeting someone they consider to be important or famous. I've seen people take on new personalities at events when a well-known leader shows up. Being someone you are not is not the way to build a strong network.

12. Be patient.

When you network with people, do so from a mindset of abundance. That is, know that opportunities are everywhere. Don't buy into the myth of a once-in-a-lifetime networking opportunity. If you maintain an abundance mindset, interesting opportunities will come up again and again. Great people will constantly come into your life.

Think of networking like playing in the World Series. You're not going to win the whole thing in one day. It's a long road. You probably won't make it in the first go-round but you *will* make it. That's the goal to strive for.

Most of your networking experience will involve taking time, going through the ebb and flow of life, realizing that it's not as easy as you originally thought it would be. Sometimes you will encounter what appears to be an opportunity, but then it doesn't quite work out. Don't force it. Be patient, and wait for a better opportunity. Allow yourself the time to develop your skill and expertise as a networker. When a good opportunity comes your way, accept it. When the opportunity isn't right, just relax and let it go.

13. Realize that the rules change once you're in.

When you finally connect and make it into the world of a busy leader, your status will likely change, and the leader's shield will go down when he or she is communicating with you. Once you've established a solid friendship, the rules change. Now your intention shifts from, "How can I begin the relationship?" to "How can I grow the relationship in the years to come?"

It's still important that you respect the leader's time. Almost all the busy people I know experience periods when too many demands are being placed upon their lives. There are times to push and there are times to pull back. Busy people are usually tight with their time in some areas but much looser in other areas. The busy leader who sends you a one-line e-mail to save a few minutes may have no qualms "shooting the breeze" with you for hours under different circumstances.

The key is to get to know the people you network with—the busy people and the not-so-busy people. Get to know their likes and dislikes. Find out their interests and share them authentically when you can. As often as possible, communicate through channels they enjoy. Through the process of time, you will develop significant, long-term, mutually beneficial relationships with people nearby and people around the globe.

You will build a net that works.

10

Evaluate Your Communication

In every aspect of life, communication is key, whether it be in marriage, among our friends, in our ministry, or in networking with others. If you have poor communication you will likely have poor leadership. I do not know of one great networking leader who is not, at the same time, an excellent communicator.

When it comes to communication, it takes "different strokes for different folks," as the saying goes. This applies not only to how people relate to one another but also to the methods and manner in which one person conveys ideas to others, whether in professional meetings, sermons, presentations, brainstorming sessions, or one-on-one chats. There are as many ways to communicate as there are speakers, audiences, and circumstances.

Still, there are some things that are true for all communicators and all communications. What makes a great communicator? What constitutes effective communication? I believe there are at least twenty keys that apply across every communication.

1. Content

You can't substitute style for substance. Every great communicator has something of value to say. They champion a cause. We've all heard presenters who have substance and no style. The result is boredom. Style is important. However, style without substantial content is a waste of everyone's time. A great communicator has the ability to bring both substance and style together for powerful communication.

2. Compassion

People matter. To great communicators, people matter greatly. You may love to speak to people, but if you don't love the people you speak to, your communication will fail. You can't be like the pastor who shared privately with a friend, "The preaching I don't mind; it's the people I can't stand." If you're going to interact with key individuals in the Body of Christ and develop a strong, vibrant, global network, you're going to have to have a passion. You must have a passion for people, a passion for the cause, and a passion that is bigger than life itself.

3. Courage

Great communicators are those who have the courage to go against conventional wisdom. They have the courage to stand up and be heard. Sometimes you are popular and sometimes you are not. You speak because you know it's the right thing to do. Over time, you will build your courage to be able to articulate your message regardless of the size of your audience.

4. Credibility

Truly great communicators practice what they preach. The Scripture is true, your sin will find you out. Once credibility is gone, almost all influence is gone with it. The higher the credibility, the higher the conviction. The higher the respect, the higher the revenue.

5. Preparedness

Great communicators have a great working knowledge of their subject matter. They rarely, if ever, wing it. Consistent study makes for ever-ready preparedness. I've often said, "What looks easy on the outside is hard on the inside." We study ourselves to death and pray ourselves back to life again. If you're going to work with global-minded, Kingdom-minded people, the fastest way to turn them off is to show up unprepared, with nothing intelligent to say. Even worse is to whitewash over a subject that you simply do not know.

6. Notes

Great communicators speak from the heart, not from the notebook. Breaking from pre-determined notes with conviction, compelling the audience to join in, is a hallmark of a great communicator. This is not to say that you cannot have notes in your public speeches, your board meetings, or in meetings with various networkers. The key is to not be glued to the notes. You have to be focused on the people.

7. Concise

Great communicators are able to take complex information and condense it into a riveting thirty-minute message. Most long-winded messages are an attempt to inform, not to connect. It is better to fall short than go too long. It is better to get to the essence quickly than say more about less. Be clear. Be simple. Be concise.

8. Convicting

Great communicators give more than a simple message. They give a passionate, convicting invitation to their listeners to do something with what they've heard. The deeper the conviction, the higher the commitment.

9. Self-Revealing

Great communicators are real with their listeners. They avoid ego-filled, self-absorbed statements and instead share real-life struggles once they have conquered the issues. Great communicators are not looking for sympathy; rather, they're hoping that what they've learned through struggles along the way may benefit others on a similar journey. Plastic people turn off great people. To be a great communicator, you must have integrity in your life and authenticity in your communication. The higher the integrity, the higher the inspiration.

10. Confidence

Confidence is not the absence of fear but moving forward in spite of it. When we were just beginning the Billion Soul

Network, I often wondered, "Would anybody else buy into this? Would anybody else follow? Would anybody else want to get involved?" It took confidence to believe in the mission and communicate it effectively with others, at a time when many others had yet to get on board.

11. Contemporary

Great communicators understand their audience's communication preferences. If you have a limited knowledge of your audience, ask others who know them. Watch other communicators. What may be effective in one place may not be effective in another. What may apply in the West may not apply in the East. We'll get more into cross-cultural communication later in this chapter.

12. Tone

Great communicators know their audience is listening to every breath so they make every syllable count. It has been said that 54 percent of what we communicate is based upon the visual, 39 percent is based upon the vocal, and the remaining 7 percent is made up of the actual words that we choose. It is important that you come across with the right tone. Great communicators make sure that every word and every nuance has power behind it.

13. Story-Telling

All of history's great communicators have been able to tell amazing stories. Fact or fiction has little to do with this ability. It is the painting of pictures in people's minds and hearts that helps them to see and understand. As we said in Chapter 4, people's minds are not debating halls but picture galleries. People don't come to hear reasons. They come to see visions.

14. Props

Most great communicators use props. While in the moment, a microphone stand can represent anything from a fireman's pole to a golf club. This type of creativity is generally spontaneous. The better the metaphors, the greater the motivation.

15. Humor

Great communicators have a very well-developed sense of humor and it shows. They know how to build on moments of hilarity without losing their audience. When you've been teaching for a while on a deep topic, it's important that you bring your people up for air, and humor is one of the fastest ways to do this. It gives your audience a chance to breathe and relax, which then allows them to absorb more teaching.

16. Pausing

Great communicators often pause in order to give their audience a moment to digest important information. There is power in the pause. Give time for people to think during your message or presentation.

17. Great Eye Contact

Good communicators make good eye contact so that each person in the audience feels as though the speaker is looking right at them. Personally, I like to find five or six people scattered throughout the audience, from left to right and from front to back, and make a conscious effort to look at them throughout my message. Then, the rest of the audience feels as if I am looking at them as well.

18. Intensity

Great communicators deliver a message with intensity. Volume and speed have little to do with it. When the heart is convicted, intensity is the aftermath. In other words, if you don't feel it, forget it. If you don't have conviction, walk away. It is not better to fake it; it is better to forget it.

19. Movement

Great communicators know that 55 percent of what they say is interpreted through body movement, so they speak more with their bodies than with their words. Your presentation begins as soon as you step in front of people, long before you open your mouth to speak the first syllable.

20. Decisions

A great communicator demands a response. He or she calls for specific and personal decisions and directions. Under a great speaker's influence, people are compelled to make a decision, to make a change, and to move forward in their lives.

Networking in Professional Settings

If you're building a network, you're going to have to communicate in a wide variety of professional settings. Yes, you will have opportunities to speak to large audiences. But you will also have to meet in many small as well as large groups. You will have to communicate with the members and workers in your network. You will have to facilitate brainstorming sessions, conduct interviews, and meet with people one-one-one. It's important to consider a number of key factors as you move ahead.

1. Setting the Agenda

Meetings need to be controlled in order to avoid wasting your time and everyone else's. For this reason, when you decide to call a meeting, the first thing you must do is identify the purpose and put together an agreed-upon agenda ahead of time. Distribute the agenda at least one day before the scheduled event. Pre-publishing the purpose and agenda of the meeting offers two main benefits. The first is that it prepares the attendees mentally and ensures that they will all arrive with a common knowledge of the topic; they will show up knowing what will be discussed and how much time has been allotted for the discussion. The second is that it allows each person to assess for themselves if it is appropriate to attend the meeting. The decision to attend or not then rests with them.

2. Choosing Attendees

Keep meetings to a manageable number of attendees. An optimal size for a small group meeting is eight participants, especially when the main purpose of the meeting is decision-making. It is best that stake-holders are informed of decisions only after the decisions have been made.

Oftentimes, too many attendees spoil the session. For one thing, inviting too many people usually means that some will not be as well-informed and will therefore be less willing to listen or less able to discuss the topic intelligently. For another thing, adding just one more person to a meeting changes the dynamics of the group and the mechanics of the communication. There are some things you will talk about when certain people are in the room, and there are some things you *won't* talk about when certain people are in the room.

3. Qualifying Lieutenant Attendees

As a networker, you may find that you want to include some of your key lieutenants or team members in a scheduled meeting. Since they are likely to be coming in at the last minute, make sure you have taken the time to keep them informed on the topic. And remember, every time you add a person to the group—even if that person is a key team member—it changes the dynamics and mechanics of the meeting.

4. Controlling the Discussion

Focus is very important in meetings, so always keep the meeting's purpose in mind, and do not lose control of the agenda. There will be occasions where an attendee asks a question not related to the discussion. Take such topic-changing questions offline. Recently, when I was conducting a roundtable near Washington, D.C., a person asked a question that had absolutely nothing to do with the theme or the topic of the day. I politely said, "I'm sorry, that has nothing to do with why we're here today. If you wish to connect with me after the meeting, we can try to do so." When you stick to the topic, you demonstrate to everyone that you respect their time and appreciate their attendance.

5. Brainstorming

Brainstorming is one of the best ways to discover outstanding ideas and find solutions to tough problems. Innovative ideas bubble up in an open environment. During a brainstorming meeting, it's important to begin by simply listing ideas; don't take time to fully assess them all. As the facilitator, avoid showing bias. Don't chastise out-of-the-box ideas. This will dampen the participants' innovativeness and creativity. Ideas that other participants find disagreeable can be set aside in a "parking lot." Don't be too quick to dismiss any idea; rather, look for other good ideas that may be generated from it. There is no such thing as a stupid idea as long as it is realistic enough to be implemented later.

Don't be too quick to dismiss any idea; rather, look for other good ideas that may be generated from it. There is no such thing as a stupid idea as long as it is realistic enough to be implemented later.

Afterwards, keep all the participants informed of the results of the brainstorming session. Tell them the steps that are going to be taken in response to the gathered ideas. If you ask for ideas but you never implement any of them, then the people will not feel that their time was appreciated. This doesn't mean that you have to do something with every idea. But if some of the group's ideas are implemented, then the participants will be able to say, "My words matter. My opinion counts."

6. Setting Direction

Setting direction for your network is a major communication responsibility but it is not the sole responsibility of the top leadership. Direction is something that the entire networking organization should understand, participate in, and remember. This does not require a complicated discussion if the network knows where to go, when to get there, how to get there, and what to do to get there. Once direction has been set, the network is ready to be put into action. Sometimes, it can be helpful to make a graphic of the direction and post it in places where the members can see it and be reminded of it.

Direction should be aligned with your own personal and mission objectives for the network; this will eventually lead to higher re-productivity. If and when significant business changes must be implemented, set aside time to make the necessary revisions to your direction. After all, having the right direction will allow you to reach the right destination.

7. Solving Problems

A problem clearly stated is a problem half-solved. It is important to go beyond the symptoms to get to the root cause of whatever problem your network is facing. Once the root cause has been identified, it will be easier to solve the problem. Don't attack the person or people involved. Stay focused on the problem.

After you define the problem, consider all the possible solutions that will best solve it. Make a list of potential courses of action and think each one through to its likely consequences. Each choice you consider should be realistic and based on the facts of the situation.

8. Listening

Listening is not just about learning the details of a problem and coming up with solutions. It's about the journey of arriving at solutions. An efficient listener is not necessarily an effective one. An efficient listener may know the details, diagnose the problem, and come up with solutions in a short time; but an effective listener will allow the other person to talk and to take a journey. He or she will listen to the other person's feelings as well as to the details of the problem. An effective listener will provide input but not formulate the solution for the other person. Otherwise, the sense of ownership of the solution is lost, and it will most likely fail for that reason.

Listening is hard work. Here are a few pointers.

- Create a good climate for talking and listening by providing a comfortable environment.
- Sit comfortably at a table and make the other person feel that he or she is the most important person on your calendar and that nothing will interrupt your discussion.
- Help articulate the problem. Show patience rather than frustration if the person has trouble explaining the problem because of negative emotions.
- Assist with problem solving. Don't plunge in and do it all yourself.
- Help the person internalize the problem, allowing him or her to make the discovery and devise the solution.
- Be empathetic and show sincere concern.
- Don't allow your own concerns to be a distraction. It's better to schedule the meeting for another time than to be distracted when you should be listening.

9. Updates

Updates are an important form of communication designed to inform various leaders in your network of the results of networking efforts, without focusing on the details of the activities behind them. Update reports should instead focus on key indicators, milestones, risks, issues, and outcomes. Some people commit the mistake of putting in all the details of a particular effort, which often leads a busy leader to ignore the entire communication for lack of time to read it all. Complete, straightforward, timely, concise, and brief status reports should only take a minute or two to read.

10. Presentations

Presentations can often be used to inform, to sell, to influence, to communicate, and to motivate people. However, the main objective of a presentation is to educate the attendees and help change their mind about a subject. Catching and keeping their attention is not easy. You really need to captivate them in the first

90 seconds. So be provocative. Start with a compelling teaser, give a summary of what you want your attendees to learn, or tell them exactly what you want them to take away. Entertaining an audience facilitates the conveyance of ideas. Use some of the communication keys we've already talked about. Allow your personality to shine through. Be passionate about your topic. Throw in a little humor and move around while maintaining good eye contact. Do not be afraid to vary your voice, speed, intonation, and volume.

11. One-on-One Meetings

Respect is an important issue when you're dealing one-on-one with "mountains of ministry" and other key leaders in the Christian world. That's why, from time to time, I have boarded a plane and flown to another country on the other side of the planet for a two-hour meeting with a single leader. By my willingness to go to such lengths, I have communicated to those leaders how much I respect them; and because I have come so far, I have their undivided attention. The saying, "First impressions last," also applies when presenting yourself to someone face-to-face.

12. Interviews

An interview is simply a form of connecting with another person, often one-on-one. The key to success is simple: Do your research. With the access we have to information technology, it's easier than ever to find out what we need to know about a particular leader or organization. You will impress the leaders you want to network with if you show them that you know a lot or at least something about them, their organizations, and their networks. If possible, talk to someone who already knows the person or who works in the organization that you want to partner with. This is a good way to confirm your ideas about the person or organization and to gauge whether or not you really want to follow through and pursue a networking relationship.

If you're seeking a specific leadership role in an organization, know as much as you can about the position description. Learn about the person that you're going to be speaking with. Go into the interview with some knowledge about his or her life, likes, dislikes, and interests so that you can establish a connection right up front. And by all means, make sure you dress the part. When you show up well-dressed, you're communicating a level of appreciation and respect. You will be more easily forgiven for being overdressed than underdressed.

13. Influencing Others

The true test of the networking leader is getting people to follow you when they do not have to follow you. If you want to communicate in a way that influences people and encourages them to follow you on your networking journey, avoid these barriers:

- Arrogance; claiming to know everything
- Indecisiveness; not sticking to the decisions that are made
- Disorganization; asking for the same information multiple times, which leads to frustration for the people involved
- Stubbornness; failing to listen to other team members or other people in the network, while insisting that others listen to you
- Negativism; a pessimistic attitude that cannot motivate others
- Cowardice; failing to admit mistakes and passing the blame to others
- Untrustworthiness; unable to gain the confidence of others due to a lack of necessary wisdom, skills, and decision-making capacity

This aspect of influencing others is very important to each of us as networkers, because God has called us to be leaders of men and women. If we're able to lead, influence, and motivate, then we will be able to build a network that mobilizes people in a greater capacity in the years to come.

14. Sharing

People who strive to be good communicators want to help others to be good communicators. That is why, in 2009, I wrote *Gutenberg to Google: The Twenty Indispensable Laws of Communication,* which is a much more complete discussion of effective communication for preachers and speakers. It is my sincere hope and prayer that leaders, pastors, and networkers everywhere learn to become effective communicators.

If you are an effective communicator, share your techniques and tools and tips. We learn from one another. Remember, when we add value, we become valuable. What better way is there to build a great network than to become valuable to many?

Networking Across Cultures

Knowing the twenty keys to great communication is foundational. Every networker can benefit from incorporating them into virtually any communication opportunity. Knowing how to communicate in various professional settings is important for the networker as well. Master networkers must take their communication skills a step further. They must learn how to communicate *cross-culturally.* Can you imagine the different kinds of cultures that you will come in contact with in the years ahead as you build your global network? Can you imagine the diversity and uniqueness that people from different cultures will bring to your networking table of ideas?

Can you imagine the diversity and uniqueness that people from different cultures will bring to your networking table of ideas?

For a networker, effective cross-cultural communication is essential. Of course, if you network in countries outside your own, you are going to deal with other cultures. But even within single nations (including the United States), many different cultures are often represented. Misunderstandings and difficulties can arise not only from language differences but also from cultural differences. As a result, many people feel disconnected from others because communication has not been as sensitive or effective as it could be.

There is no simple recipe for communicating smoothly and effectively with people from other countries and cultures. However, there are five essential elements that can get you started in the right direction.

1. Questions

Be courageous and ask incisive questions. Why courageous? First, many people feel stupid when they need to ask questions. They think that asking a question infers that they're not clever enough to understand. Second, many people are wary of being politically incorrect. They're afraid that their questions will be interpreted wrongly. Take courage and ask. Only questions will drive the understanding necessary to help you make strong connections and forge good networking relationships. When you ask a question, you are not showing ignorance or misinterpretation; you are testing your understanding.

2. Attention

Give full attention with all of your senses. Be alert to the nuances of verbal and non-verbal communication that have vast and varying differences across cultures. Listen with your eyes and hear with your heart.

3. Clarification

Check for understanding by summarizing what you think you have heard or understood, even at the risk of someone being affronted or thinking that you're not so bright. Remaining silent and being faced with the consequences of being misinformed or uninformed is much worse. If necessary, consult other people for clarification. Most people are only too pleased to help with communication in their culture when someone shows a genuine interest in learning. This can be especially important when it comes to humor. If you're in a different country and you want to be humorous in a presentation, run your humorous story or anecdote by someone from that culture first. If they do not laugh, don't try to tell the joke to a larger audience.

4. Limitations

Openly acknowledge your relative ignorance or limitations when it comes to other people's beliefs, values, or culture norms and explain how this might make you appear clumsy in your communication. If you don't, you're either hoping that (1) your ignorance doesn't exist, or (2) that it will not be noticed. Experience dictates that neither is usually the case. The good news is, most people will accept and respond to your honest discomfort with consideration and respect and use the situation to teach you something about their culture.

5. Value

Recognize that diversity is a source of abundance and a cause for celebration in your global network. To create synergy and value from cross-cultural interactions is the approach of all effective intercultural dialogues. Remember, there is no communication until each party understands the other. Effective cross-cultural communication is about testing understandings and assumptions and managing each other's expectations. It's about relating to people in a respectful way, no matter what their roots or where they're from. It's a craft and a skill that can be learned and your networking success will depend largely upon how well you master it.

Summary Questions

I have presented a lot of information in this chapter. Clearly, communication is the key to effective networking and great communication has many facets. Still, there are some over-arching questions that you and I can ask ourselves as we evaluate our communication as networkers. These four questions are critical. If you can answer "yes" to all four of them, you are well on your way to becoming a great communicator.

- **Is it clear?**

At the Billion Soul Network we strive to make everything we say, write, and publish as clear as possible. Before we step in front of an audience or send material out the door, we bounce the communication off of as many people as we possibly can to make sure the goal is clear and the flow is in the right direction. If it is not clear to you, if it is not clear to your immediate circle, it will not be clear to your readers or hearers. In order to build a strong and growing network, it is imperative that your communication be clear.

- **Is it concise?**

Just because you know a lot about the subject doesn't mean that you have to speak or write a lot about the subject. Communication experts tell us that people who understand a topic write less, not more. Get your missional statement down to its very essence—fifteen or twenty words or less. Don't speak forty minutes when twenty minutes would be more effective. That's taking the easy way out.

- **Is it convincing?**

As we said in the first chapter, if you don't answer the "why" question, you'll never get to the "wow!" You must answer "why." Until you do so convincingly, you don't have a cause. You don't have anything of value for people to believe in. If you want to have a buy-in, you must have a believe-in. If people do not *believe in*, they will never *buy in*. And if they don't buy in, they won't be motivated—they won't be motivated to be inconvenienced, they won't be motivated to follow, and they won't be motivated to move forward with you in the vision and mission God has given to you.

- **Is it compelling?**

Does it stir the soul? Does it harness the heart? Does it captivate a man or woman's imagination? Can they see greatness in what you're sharing? Can they understand the value that your vision will bring to their lives and the value they could add to the lives of others?

The fact is, if God has called you to build a network and lead men and women to work together toward a Great Commission goal, then becoming a great communicator is a necessary part of that calling. Take the time to evaluate your communication. Learn from others. Develop your skills. With God's help, you can become a communicator who changes lives and changes the world.

Enlist Your Comrades

What is it going to take to make your network work? What will it take for your vision to move beyond the realm of daydream to become not only a reality, but a force in the world? The answer is simple: it's going to take a lot of effective people.

I don't know where you may be living as you read this. I don't know if your home is in a tropical or non-tropical environment. Currently I live on the Space Coast in the Sunshine State of Florida, but I came here by way of Springfield, Missouri. So, I have seen snow. In the northern part of the Northern Hemisphere, we get snow. Snowstorms always illustrate for me the networking potential of a person or an organization.

If one snowflake falls in Chicago, Illinois, for example, no one pays attention. One snowflake means nothing in Chicago. Even if a flurry of snowflakes falls in Chicago, windshield wipers on automobiles just knock them off and people go on with their lives and their work. However, when billions and billions of snowflakes fall in Chicago, those snowflakes together make a statement that no single snowflake can make. The collective force of billions of snowflakes says, "Schools are closed and students can stay home today," or, "The airport is shut down, so no flights can go in or out." One snowflake cannot say that. Billions of snowflakes can.

All I am is one snowflake. All you are is one snowflake. By ourselves, we can't say much and we definitely can't achieve much. But together, collectively, with many other people joining us, we can do something.

At the time of this writing, there are over 1.3 billion Protestant Christians in the world. That's a lot of snowflakes. If God's people would simply learn to work together, what could a blizzard of such size and magnitude accomplish in the next handful of years? If we, the people of God, were able to double our number just one time in ten years—if each of us won just one person to Christ— we would go from 1.3 billion Protestant Christians to 2.6 billion Protestant Christians in one decade. Then, if ten years from now we decided to do it again, there would be 5.2 billion Protestant Christians—and the whole world will have heard the glorious Gospel of Jesus Christ. The glory of the Lord would cover the earth like the water covers the sea. One snowflake can't do that, but billions and billions of snowflakes can.

You can't do much with one grain of sand; but a master sculptor can take trillions of grains of sand and craft them into beautiful sandcastles and marvelous figures. One grain of sand can't create much of a picture, but billions of grains of sand can. One little string can't make a net of any value to a fisherman; but many knots created by tying hundreds or even thousands of strings together can bring in an amazing catch.

That's the power of enlisting your comrades.

If God's people would simply learn to work together, what could a blizzard of such size and magnitude accomplish in the next handful of years?

Think back to Abraham's servant, Eleazar, in Genesis 24. To accomplish his mission, he was going to need help, both from the physical world and the spiritual world. He was going to need angelic power and the assistance of many people along the way. He was going to need the favor of God and the favor of the people he met in order to bring a bride back for Isaac. If you and I are ever going to get the Bride and the Bridegroom together, we're going to have to enlist a lot of people.

As I have said before, small dreams never enflamed the hearts of great people. If we want to have great people in our lives and our networks, we're going to have to be attractive in ways that draw them toward us. There is an art to inviting people to join us on our networking journey. In the New Testament, Jesus usually called His disciples one by one; sometimes He called a couple at a time. But He always said, "Follow Me, and I will make you fishers of men." In other words, "I'm going to give you a higher cause for living. I'm going to give you a purpose and a mission in life greater than you ever imagined." The disciples responded by leaving their old ways of life and following Jesus on the greatest global mission of all time.

How should you go about inviting people to participate in your network? What are the best ways to enlist your comrades? Whether your network is just in its beginning stages or has been around for some time, I believe the following steps are an effective guide. They are steps that we have used in the development of the Billion Soul Network, which has grown from the vision of two individuals into a movement involving over 450,000 churches worldwide.

Looking at the Strategic Picture

One of the main goals for inviting leaders to participate in a network is to tie relational knots. As these knots mature, many will become powerful hubs for ministry. However, not all knots are the same nor should they be approached in the same way. Just as there are different kinds of knots with different purposes, as any Boy Scout or sailor will tell you, so there are diverse kinds of relational knots.

While this is not an exhaustive list, most relational knots fall into certain self-explanatory categories, such as geographic, missional, communicational, educational, financial, or niche-oriented. Overarching all of these is one more category: *strategic*. Tying strategic knots involves stepping back, observing our networking landscape, and then deciding what kinds of knots we need to tie. Where do we need new knots? Who do we need to tie in and what is the best time, place and method for connecting them? How can we tie all of our different kinds of knots together in a way that works toward our greater purpose?

When striving to tie a strategic knot, it is always best to connect similar kinds of people. For example, inviting a person with a conservative mindset into a group of risk takers will most likely not turn out well. The risk-averse individual will probably be uncomfortable in the group and eventually drop out. Yet, if some forethought had been given to the best place and the best way to tie this person into the network, he or she could have been nurtured into a powerful ally.

Strategic knot-tying is a lot like playing the game of chess. Master networkers must always be thinking two or three moves ahead. Which knot should you tie first, second, and third? If you invite this person first, will that open a door for you to invite the next person? Will tying this knot here create an opportunity for you to tie that knot there?

1. Invite People Progressively

Here is what I mean: Maybe twice a year or once a quarter, take time to think of individuals that you believe need to be invited to participate in your network. These would be people you believe could have a role in the fulfillment of your network's goals. Make a list and then organize the names in a logical, sequential order. Don't randomly go about your business, inviting this person or that person, fatalistically believing that your network will somehow come together. Take the people you believe are the busiest or the most difficult to gain access to and put them at the end of the list. Then begin inviting those you believe you can most easily reach and ramp up from there. Eventually you will create a "domino effect" that will put you in a position to contact and get the attention of those leaders you originally considered out of reach.

There is an art and a science to inviting progressively so that top leaders come to see that your network is worthy of their time. One of the main ways that leaders make this assessment is by knowing who else is already involved. They think, "If I get involved, I will be able to interface with this person or that person who is already in the network." By having other key people already on board, your network is more attractive to those leaders who are very busy or are perhaps more renowned.

2. Invite People Purposefully

Be very specific in your invitation. Show that you have assessed who the people are and that you recognize their skills, talents, and the value they could bring to the network as well as the value that could be reciprocated back to them. Invite them with a specific purpose in mind. There truly are riches in niches. When you appeal to people's individual gifts or strengths, you are respecting them and the gifts that God has given them. People respond more quickly and positively to such an appeal as opposed to a general invitation that doesn't acknowledge the value they would add. Great people do want to add value to other people.

When you appeal to people's individual gifts or strengths, you are respecting them and the gifts that God has given them.

3. Invite People Privately

There are times when it is best to invite a leader privately. Early in 2011, I made a key connection. I knew that one well-known Christian leader who lived in the central United States had a fond appreciation for another renowned leader who lived outside the country. The American leader appreciated the other leader's ministry, family, and legacy. The Lord allowed me the privilege of arranging a meeting where the three of us could get together. It was done privately and in a way that allowed both leaders to feel appreciated and respected.

When you invite people to participate in your network privately, approach them with a specific mission and a specific goal. Communicate how you believe they can uniquely add value and fill a void in the network. Great people don't want to waste anyone's time and they certainly don't want to waste their own. They want every minute to be compounded; they want their life to count. By inviting them purposefully and privately, you show that you respect and appreciate them.

4. Invite People Professionally

If you're going to have a one-on-one meeting, be on time. Go to the location the day before, if possible, and mark out your map, so you know exactly how to get there and how long it will take you. If you're going to be late for some reason, call ahead and let the person know you're going to be late. Do not fail to show up without having notified the person ahead of time. Don't be a no-show. You're communicating on many different levels and what you're saying isn't good. I realize there could be an exception to this rule; a crisis may come your way and you may have no choice. But 99 percent of the time, given the technological world in which we live, you can find some way to get word to the person.

Be professional. Be professional in the way you go about getting ready for the meeting. Be professional when you are there and professional when you leave. Be sure to follow up the meeting with correspondence and do whatever you have promised. Whatever is worth starting is worth finishing. If it's not worth finishing, don't start. You don't want to become known as a person who begins things but quits before they are finished or who does not follow through on scheduled plans and dates.

I have been on the receiving end of a person who chose to be a no-show without letting me know. When that person called later wanting to reschedule, I was reluctant to set another date. It wasn't an issue of anger or resentment or unforgiveness; it was just that I believe I must steward my life in a way that is pleasing to the Lord. I don't believe God desires for any of us to waste our time on people who do not follow through on what they begin.

5. Invite People Publicly

There are times and circumstances when it is best to privately invite individuals to get involved in your network. There are also times when it is best to invite people publicly.

Each year our network holds Billion Soul Summits throughout the United States and around the world. We spend a lot of time inviting key people to come and bring presentations. We invite them publicly. We promote that they're going to be with us. Some of these individuals are deeply involved in the network; some are acquaintances of the network. Some are people we've broken bread with who have become intimate friends. Some are individuals we're looking forward to getting to know with the hope that they will want to become involved in the network in a deep and vibrant way.

6. Invite People Practically

Not everyone in the world is going to want to get involved in your network, and not everyone should. Be practical as you consider who you should invite and who you should not invite.

Everyone is redeemable but not everyone is teachable. Years ago, when I interviewed Robert Schuler in his Los Angeles office, I asked him what he thought the greatest three truths were for the next generation. His first response was, "Humility." When I asked him why, he said, "Because humility is the gateway to teachability."

The opposite of humility is arrogance. If you notice that someone is arrogant, he or she is probably not teachable or networkable. They're not the kind of person you want to spend extra time with. If a person is extreme in an area of theology—say, he or she has a very narrow view of who's going to Heaven—then you probably don't want to have that person in your network either. If someone spends a lot of time being critical of others in the Body of Christ who are genuinely redeemed, that person is probably not networkable.

By inviting people practically, we are able to network successfully without adding unnecessary stress. That's what we try to do at Billion Soul Network. We strive to network from the middle, from a belief system that empowers and compounds the effectiveness of the people that choose to participate with us.

7. Invite People Positively

When you invite people to get involved in your network, you want to invite them to a positive experience, a positive environment, and a positive, energetic way of life. You can do this by demonstrating to them that the invitation is positive in three ways.

Value. Show them that their value will be compounded in the lives of many and value will be compounded back to them. Let them know that if they have a valuable resource that should be made available for sale in the network, you will rev-share that value back to them.

Vision. Demonstrate time and time again what the vision is; repeat it over and over. Help people to see that their involvement will help fulfill the vision because they have a part in God's heart. There is a niche that only they can fulfill. Regardless of what stream of Christianity they are from, they have a God-given uniqueness in the Body of Christ.

Victory. Show them that victory *will* come. Articulate that you do have a roadmap for success. Prove that you have a system and a process to follow that will ensure growth and success in the future.

8. Invite People Persuasively

There are too many prognosticators and procrastinators in our world today. There are too many people who say, "Someday," but "someday" is basically "no day." You don't find "someday" on the calendar. "Someday" is not one of the days of the week. "Someday" is a fictitious day, a fantasy day. As networkers, we're not about "someday." We're about *today.* We must be persuasive!

I remember when I traveled to New Zealand to interview Sir Edmund Hillary, the great explorer who was the first man to climb Mount Everest. The date was August 31, 2007. I found Sir Edmund to be a captivating, insightful, diligent, and wise man. We were discussing various aspects of life and the opportunities that life brings us when I asked him to explain something. "You told me that once we decide what our life's project is going to be, we should start *now.* Why should we start now? I do believe that procrastination has damned more souls to hell than anything else. Why do you say, 'Start now?'"

He looked at me and responded, "I'm 88 years old and there are six projects that I will not be able to finish." I assumed he meant six small projects—maybe a book project, cleaning out the attic, or taking care of other small things before he graduated for eternity. (In fact, he went on to be with the Lord a few months later.)

"Would you share with us one of those projects that you don't believe you will be able to complete?" I asked.

"I was the first one to climb Mount Everest," he said. "I was also the first one to cross Antarctica. In 1955, I was crossing Antarctica and I climbed up to the top of a high mountain range. When I looked from the top of that mountain range down into the valley below, I saw the glacier filled with animal life and then another mountain range on the other side. I said to myself, 'Sir Edmund, hike down this mountain, crawl across that ice, climb the other mountain, and see what is on the other side.' But then I also said, 'I'm young. I have plenty of time. I'll come back and do it another day.'

We all have two seasons in our life. We have a season when time and energy work for us, and we have a season when time and energy work against us.

"James," he continued, "I'm too old now. I will never be able to go back to Antarctica. I will never be able to crawl across the ice and climb the other mountain range and see the view from the bottom of the earth. I'm just too old." Then he added these words of wisdom that I will never forget. "There are two seasons in every person's life," he said. "There is a season when time and energy work *for* you and there is a season when time and energy work *against* you. You do not know what season you're in until you attempt a project bigger than yourself."

While I was there, I had three books autographed by Sir Edmund Hillary. As I watched his hand shake as he wrote my name and the date inside each book, I realized that time and energy were working against him so much that holding a pen and signing his name was a difficult challenge; and yet, there was a season in his life when those same hands compelled him to climb sheer walls of ice on the steep trek to the top of Mount Everest and across the bottom of the earth in Antarctica!

We all have two seasons in our life. We have a season when time and energy work for us, and we have a season when time and energy work against us. We must do the big stuff *now*. How do we do the big stuff? We can't do the big things by ourselves; they're too big. We cannot fulfill the Great Commission alone. One is too small a number for greatness. In order to achieve something God-sized, it takes all of God's people. To achieve something of global significance, it takes people all over the world. If you're going to transform your community, city, state, nation, and beyond, it's going to take a lot of people. It's going to take a lot of knot tying, relationship building, strategic thinking, and networking to make the vision become a reality.

And so we enlist our comrades. We gladly, gratefully, and graciously extend invitations to key people to become a part of something bigger than themselves. We invite them to join us as we work together to put the Cross of Jesus Christ on the roof of the world and announce once and for all that Jesus is the only way to Heaven and to eternal life. May we, as master networkers, strive to enlist our comrades, believing God to help us find the right people and give them the right assignments. That's how we will make our net work. That's how we will turn our network into net worth. That's how we will fulfill the Great Commission in our lifetime.

Let's start now!

Conclusion

Which number in 1,000,000,000 has the most value? Think your answer through carefully. If you say "the last zero," then you have answered correctly! A lot people would say "1"—but what is the 1without the last zero? The value is only 1. It is the last zero that turns 1 into a billion.

What kind of value do you wish to add? I believe this is the most important secret of all when it comes to building a net that works. This is my final challenge to you: Let's think about this "last zero" concept.

1. The last zero brings *compounding* value.

I must admit, even though I did not recognize it in my early years, one of my personal ambitions has been to add value everywhere I go to everyone I serve in ministry. With every step I have taken from the front of the line, I have chosen to compound my value into the lives of others. We live in a world where most people—even people in ministry—think that getting to the front of the line is the most important goal in life. This is the opposite of what Jesus taught His disciples. Speaking about Judgment Day, He said, "Those who are first will be last, and those who are last will be first." I watch pastors and ministers jostle for position and prestige, thinking their efforts will get them promotion and make them a little more known. Through the years I have had to step out and lead and mobilize a lot of people, but it has usually been from the position of, "Look at what I am already doing," not, "Watch me do this, so I can impress you."

In the early years of Cutting Edge International, we published a quarterly newsletter called "The Cutting Edge." Each edition was filled with sermons and sermon ideas for pastors to utilize. Many pastors told me that they always read the newsletter and filed it for future reference, and not in file thirteen to be thrown away. Every time a pastor shared this with me, it meant so much, knowing that I had added value.

Be sure to find compounding value to offer your fellow leaders. Be willing to step to the end of the line and watch your value soar.

2. The last zero brings *completing* value.

As I have already articulated in this book, networking is not about competing but completing. It is about finishing the Great Commission. There is completion in stepping to the back of the line to serve everyone before us. Why would we want to serve half when Christ has called us to serve all? As I enter the second half of my life, I find that only those things that bring completion really matter. I have heard it said, "Legacy is what we set in motion for the next generation." I realize there are elements of truth in this statement; but I am not as interested in starting something as I am in completing what I start. This is not to say that our personal value cannot extend into the next generation. In fact, it should. But I don't want to be remembered for the loose ends I left behind; I want to be remembered for the knots that I tied. If you are going to start something, then strive to complete it!

3. The last zero brings *compassion* value.

It has been said countless times, "People will not care how much you know until they know how much you care." This is true for starters. But as networkers, we want to go further than this.

Not long ago, I was walking along with a young Hindu gentleman in Indonesia. He was so pleasant to talk to! I asked him if he was familiar with Jesus Christ and the local church in his city. He said that he was.

"Have you ever considered following Christ?" I asked.

"No," he answered. "I am a Hindu."

When I heard those words, my heart immediately went out to this very lost soul. I looked into his eyes and said, "I challenge you go to a local church and hear the man of God share Christ." He said that he would do so. I sure hope that he followed through.

How long can your love last? How far can it reach? Can you develop a love for all peoples and all ethnics and all nations? Your network will never be any larger than the width and depth of your love for people, both saved and lost.

4. The last zero brings *consequential* value.

Our Lord and Savior Jesus Christ taught that we will reap according to how much we sow. What is appalling to me is to see fellow ministers who want to add a value of ten and expect a billion in return. This may not be what they preach, but it's what they practice. It is high time for us to get off WIFM (What's In It For Me?) and get on WIFJ (What's In It For Jesus?)

We can choose our choices but not our consequences. The consequences are in the reaping hands of God. The late Dr. Bill Bright, founder of Campus Crusade for Christ, once told me that he would call three to five people each day to pray for them. He shared that his custom was to have his quiet time with the Lord, followed by reaching out to people who could do very little for him in return. He practiced this until the very end of his life. Think about the value of this over the years in the lives of people!

Being the last zero has unparalleled consequences. Each day missed in adding value makes it that much harder to reach the billion-times value at the end of life's journey.

5. The last zero brings *complex* value.

How can serving others be complex or complicated? First of all, sometimes people can misread us. They may wonder, "Why does he defer to others? Is he doing this for some hidden personal gain?" If someone mutters this or you happen to hear about it, simply ignore it and add value again.

Second, serving others requires us to think deeply and strategically. If we are going to add billion-times value, we need to find time to think through how we can accomplish this; we can't go about just randomly doing this and that.

Networking isn't about following a pecking order or going after the "big names." In my opinion, there are no big shots or little shots in the Kingdom of God. At the same time, if we are going to have a net that works, we can't be everywhere and do everything. We do need others—the right others. I spend a great deal of time thinking carefully about the knots that need to be tied with various people, and how adding value to these individuals will add value to the net worldwide. Since countless cultures come into play, the complexity increases over time. Each time we add another variable, the more complicated it becomes to expand the network in a way that truly adds value to everyone in it.

6. The last zero brings *Christian* value.

We have now come back to the place where we started so many pages ago. When Christ spoke to Peter and said, "Put out into deep water and let down your nets for a catch," He was bringing a change to Peter's way of thinking and living. Peter came to comprehend that day that the value Christ brings is unprecedented and immeasurable, not only for him, but also for his fellow disciples and the people in the nearby boats.

When was the last time that your godly influence caused others to cast their nets into deeper water? To stop doing things the way they have always done them and start doing them in the "last zero" kind of way? If we are going to finish the Great Commission and fill this world with Christ, then all of us are going to have do things differently. We're going to have to stop caring about who gets the credit as long as Christ gets the glory.

We can do it! It will be done! We are winning the next billion in our generation. Let's tie synergistic knots that will make our net work for the fulfillment of the Great Commission. Let's believe the Lord for a harvest so great that our nets begin to break, and for hearts large enough to share the catch with the pastors and churches around us.

1

The Global Networked Church

We are living in an era when every local church can truly be networked together with numerous local churches and organizations to help fulfill the Great Commission. One of the greatest marks of a global networked church is not just *seating* capacity but *sending* capacity. Can you imagine how fast Christianity would flourish throughout the earth if just 1,000 churches would send 100 missionaries out from their ranks in a ten- to twenty-year timespan? The outcome would be another 100,000 missionaries strategically placed throughout the hardest-to-reach places in the world.

Most times, when a new action principle is presented, we need a model or a living example to follow. We need to learn from someone who has already done what we want to do. When I think of the global networked Church, immediately my mind races to World Harvest Center in Suva, Fiji, founded in 1991by Pastor Suliasi Kurulo. Today, Pastor Suli leads a global networked church, synergizing with local churches and organizations in every world region. Moreover, out of the World Harvest Center, Suli has planted more than 3,000 churches in 110 nations. On any given Sunday, this global congregation exceeds 250,000. All of this has originated from one of the poorest nations on earth, not to mention one of the most remote!

What are the steps required for a local church to make the leap to become a global networked church? I believe the eleven phases delineated in this book are necessary for any local church to become globally interwoven into the fabric of faith worldwide.

1. Establish your cause.

When we move from just *having* church to *being* the church, we choose to become what the Church was intended to be. From the inception of World Harvest Center, Pastor Suli and his team have been on a trajectory course to truly help fulfill the Great Commission. While they realize that they cannot do this alone, they have made a phenomenal effort to move forward towards this goal.

2. Examine your conditions.

In the early years of the ministry, World Harvest Center faced and fought numerous challenges, from denominationalism to national politics to death in the family to finances. As it relates to finances, it has often been said by Westerners that "they" (those in less developed nations or regions) can do "all these great things" for the Lord because life is simpler in their part of the world. Yet, this could not be further from the truth. The global Church has always faced enormous challenges throughout history.

During one era in Pastor Suli's ministry, when they were building their existing church building, they ran out of money and did not know where they were going to find enough in seven days to satisfy the bank and the contractor. Without telling his congregation what they were facing, Suli went to prayer. He interceded to the Lord to provide the funds needed to complete the church project. The Holy Spirit moved upon the people to sell whatever they could (furniture, clothes, jewelry, etc.) and to give it to the building project. The people lined up as far Suli could see them, as they brought their offerings from the sales of their personal possessions. Can you even begin to imagine this?

There comes a time for all us, if we're serious about "getting the bride and bridegroom together" for the fulfillment of the Great Commission, that we must examine every area of our lives to determine where we are and what our conditions are. The entire congregation of the World Harvest Center had to evaluate what really mattered the most and then move forward with action to accomplish what seemed to be impossible.

3. Embrace your commission.

How many more goal-setting events do we need to attend? When will ever move from "missions projects" to actually thinking about how we can maximize our time, talent, and treasures to hit the target?

Pastor Suli often tells a story about attending Amsterdam 2000, the nine-day conference for preaching evangelists convoked by Dr. Billy Graham in the summer of 2000. I was fortunate to serve for more than two years on the Executive Program Committee with Dr. Graham, Dr. John Corts, Dr. Elmer Towns, and many more, as we prepared for this historic gathering of nearly 12,000 leaders from 217 nations. During Amsterdam 2000, a group of leaders got together and they gave their group a particular name. I have intentionally left the name out. Suli was in this group and he listened to various leaders as they make bold commitments to go out, engage the rest of the unreached people groups, and finish the Great Commission. Years went by, however, and Suli saw very little follow-through on these commitments. Rather than continuing to sit on the sidelines with others, Suli decided to launch a bold initiative from Suva, Fiji. The rest is now history!

Pastor Suli and the World Harvest Center have found their role in God's goal. They have become an example for the world of what it means to build a global networked church. May their tribe increase by 1,000 percent!

4. Enforce your character.

What we talk about is the evidence of what we are thinking about. Words are the outward expression of our inward thoughts. When you converse with Pastor Suli, you will hear about the Bible passage he is currently reading, the burden he is carrying, the victory he is experiencing, and the prayer he is believing the Lord to answer for him. When he talks about his family, tears well up in his eyes, demonstrating his love for his wife, children, and grandchildren.

In order to build a global networked church, we must have the kind of character that sees it through to the end. Temptations will come to take the short cut and not do it right. Nevertheless, when we finally witness the reality of having a church that is connected to the global Church, a church that is moving forward in the fulfillment of the Great Commission, we'll find that the satisfaction far outweighs the sacrifice.

Can you imagine building a global networked church in the next five years? It can be done! Suliasi Kurulo is the proof. Every pastor who chooses to make this leap out of the comfortable, traditional fish bowl of missions to land in the unfamiliar ocean of global networking will meet amazing mountains of ministry like Pastor Suli who are spanning the globe with the gospel.

5. Engage your creativity.

The more I have researched, the more I have become convinced that the most creative leaders in the Church are those who are focused on networking together for the Great Commission. It is as if the Holy Spirit deposits in their hearts and minds new and exciting ways to achieve God's goal in the earth. Pastor Suli's annual convention, with more than 8,000 who attend each year, plus tens of thousands who watch via national television and Internet, always includes:

- **Information.** Delegates hear reports from around the world, including exciting testimonies about what has happened in the last twelve months and what is happening now.
- **Inspiration.** Faith is built and motivation is increased through the worship times at the convention, as well as through the moving testimonies of new churches being planted and countless souls being saved.
- **Identification.** People are given time to pray and identify with world regions and particular missionaries that are about to leave for the foreign field. Pastor Suli believes that "identification" is an extremely important bridge for people to cross in order to get them to go on the missionary journey for the long-term.
- **Involvement.** Guest presenters are brought in each year to challenge the convention delegates. Different avenues

of action are offered, so people can decide for themselves how much time and treasure they want to commit.

- **Investment.** Delegates are asked to make an annual investment into the projects and missionaries the Lord has laid upon their hearts. Then, on the last night of the convention, new missionaries who have demonstrated proven ministry are ordained.

6. Explore your core.

We have to know what we believe and put our beliefs to work. When Suli made the commitment to launch out into the deep, he was wise enough to know that he could not accomplish God's vision for his life alone. He has methodically built a global network tied to his local church to advance the cause of Christ.

7. Equip your circle.

When you study Pastor Suli's paradigm of ministry, you discover a systematic approach to equipping key leaders on a weekly basis. Even when Suli is away speaking and ministering, his team is equipped weekly for effective ministry. All modes of communication—books, video, the Internet—are incorporated into this regularly scheduled training. Our chain will only be as strong as our weakest link.

8. Encourage your confidence.

All of us sooner or later need encouragement. Pastor Suli is no different. I have been privileged to see him up and down along the road of ministry. All of us have to find people and places to rejuvenate ourselves. Find a hobby. Spend quality time with your family. We need to make the relationship exchange away from the "withdrawals" of our life and towards the "deposits."

9. Exemplify your commitment.

Networkers help with the net! When I arrived to minister in Pastor Suli's missions convention in 2008, he handed me an envelope filled with funds to help cover my roundtrip airfare. He exemplified a sowing spirit. He didn't just talk about it.

We preach and teach our best sermons when our friends and fellow servants witness us living what we are saying. Everywhere Suli goes, he is able to share the story of the more than 3,000 churches that World Harvest Center has planted in more than 100 nations. Instead of saying, "We hope to do something great for the Lord someday," he can testify to how they have done it and how they continue to do it each week!

10. Evaluate your communication.

Over the years I have witnessed the powerful communication of Pastor Suli's ministry as well as the excellence of the materials produced through this ministry. For the sake of the long run, they have not taken short cuts. They have made sure that excellence is demonstrated in their communication throughout Fiji and around the world.

11. Enlist your comrades.

In the last few years, I have seen Pastor Suli move his entire church to the next level. Now that he has established a global presence from Fiji, he is inviting pastors and churches worldwide to partner with him and do what he has done. In other words, his example is challenging pastors to create global networked churches and to partner with him in the process. It is not either/ or but both/and. For example, when he is Latin America, he challenges the pastors to adopt specific unreached people groups not just in their region but in different places in the world. He issues the same challenge wherever he travels.

2

Traditional Missions Vs. Global Missions

I grew up in a progressive home, where my parents lived full lives and taught their children to think broadly, work hard, and believe for the best. As a family we possessed a can-do attitude with a follow-through aptitude. I believe this background prepared me to be ready for open doors and to view the world from different viewpoints.

When I left home in January 1982 to attend Central Bible College in Springfield, Missouri, I had already made some smaller decisions of "this for that" as I thought through the options before me in the light of the bigger picture that the Lord was showing me. Upon getting to Central Bible College, I was confronted with various kinds of worldviews as well as with different levels of understanding of the Church. I remember a conversation with my roommate in which I shared that I planned to preach and minister during my time in Springfield.

"You won't be able to do that since there are already so many preachers and pastors in the area," he said.

"Oh yes, I will!" I responded.

"Why are so confident?"

"Since I am willing to minister anywhere," I said, "there will always be a place for me to preach and minister."

Herein lies one of the greatest leadership secrets: If we are willing to serve anywhere, there will always be a "where" for us to serve. This is the kind of outlook that is needed to see the unseen paradigms that are before us. I have discovered that most pastors genuinely believe that they are doing global missions and helping to fulfill the Great Commission in our generation. Yet, their traditional paradigm is not adequate to help them to see what they are not seeing and learn what they were not learning. It took me years before the unseen and unlearned became seen and learned. I must confess there is still so much more that I do not know!

In order for us to move from a traditional missions paradigm to a global one, we must first adjust our mindset. The old school was primarily based on *funding* and *training*. The new school is based on *networking* and *partnering*. In other words, we have to change our missions mindset from "parenting" to "partnering." This is not as easy to achieve as we might first think. As soon as we begin to adjust, we run into missional systems that have been in place for decades and are hardened against quick revision.

For example, if your church has worked from a traditional missions viewpoint for a long time, you no doubt support a number of missionaries who primarily train and teach the national church in some region of the world. Most likely the majority of these missionaries do not live on the edge of missional endeavors among the unreached/unengaged people groups of our generation.

Dr. James Hudson Taylor IV of OMF International (formerly the China Inland Mission and Overseas Missionary Fellowship) teaches the following steps for moving from "parents" to "partners." First, we have to build relationships. There are no shortcuts here. The deeper the relationship, the shorter the distance between the idea and its execution. Second, there has to be mutual ownership. People have to see themselves in the outcome in order for them to go on the long run. Third, effective communication is paramount. Verbal and non-verbal communication must be taken into account. Fourth, we have to leverage diversity and unity. The more we can harmonize, the more we can evangelize.

Oftentimes, leaders get these first four steps right, but they miss the fifth one: we have to put in place appropriate structures and best practices. If the structures are not right, others will be unable to get plugged in to various projects. Sixth, we need motivation for God's glory and the furtherance of His kingdom. We have to keep the main things the main things! I have included a graphic below so you can see what we now teach throughout the Billion Soul Network.

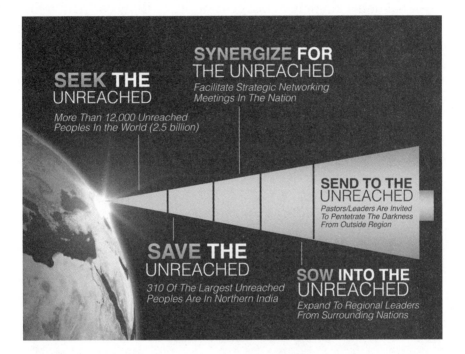

Once a local church or organization begins to make the mental shift from traditional to global missions, so many more options come into play to achieve the desire outcomes. I must confess I understood some parts of this shift, but the concept became clearer to me when Rev. Roland Vaughn, former World Missions Director for the Church of God, taught me this "Five-Point Arrowhead."

The five points of the missions arrowhead are:

- Seek the Unreached
- Save the Unreached

- Synergize for the Unreached
- Sow into the Unreached
- Send to the Unreached

This Five-Point Arrowhead depicts one of greatest shifts of missional understanding in our generation. It is my conviction that this networking paradigm will work anywhere in the world. We can see the significant differences between traditional and global missions by viewing them through the lens of the arrowhead.

Traditional Missions

Here is the Five-Point Arrowhead from the perspective of traditional missions practice.

Be sure to carefully think through both paradigms (traditional and global) as you strive to move from one to the other. Keep in mind that the global paradigm becomes easier in time, as you get to know leaders outside of your silo in various regions of the world.

1. Seek the Unreached: The missionary answers the call.

Even though I have not officially served as a missionary in the traditional sense, I have served as a missionary in the global sense for decades. Our common understanding is that people, as individuals or couples, answer the call to be missionaries and connect with their denomination or organization. Oftentimes, this calling is first perceived in their youth and fulfilled in the years that follow. The call may be general or it may focus on a specific country or people group. At other times, the denomination or organization dictates where missionaries will fulfill our God-given calling.

2. Save the Unreached: The missionary is equipped.

For decades the Bible college/seminary approach has served the Church with exceptional results. Some missional organizations require up to eight years of training before their missionaries can land their feet in a particular world region. Again, while this model has served the Church well for a long time, it faces numerous challenges in the twenty-first century. For example, with the explosion of the Internet, online training is now at the fingertips of anyone in the world.

3. Synergize for the Unreached: The missionary seeks funding.

Once missionaries have gone through a certain amount of schooling, the next step, typically, is to begin to raise the funds necessary to actually go to the "called field." This is a grueling task. As they go to various churches and people, they share their vision and invite pastors and churches to partner in their effort to provide missions to a particular world region. Depending upon their fund-raising skill and how many people they know, this funding phase can take up to two years, and sometimes more.

4. Sow into the Unreached: The missionary learns the language.

Once missionaries actually get to the field, they have to learn the language and culture in order to do effective ministry. It is not that nothing is done during this phase; but the work is limited until the language is grasped enough for effectiveness.

Regardless of whether the missions view is traditional or global, career missionaries do have to learn the language at some point, if they plan to stay in the area for any length of time.

5. Send to the Unreached: The missionary begins ministry.

Even though the missionaries have been in the field, they are only now really equipped for their assignment and able to begin multiplying ministry. How many years have elapsed since they first entered Bible college or seminary? Think about the answer for a moment. I'm not proposing that this traditional approach is evil; but this was adequate when the global church was young and not indigenous in so many regions like it is today. What has brought us this far will not by itself get us to the finish line.

Global Missions

I realize that some people will have issues with the terms "traditional missions" and "global missions." In one sense, traditional missions has taken us to global missions. Yet, going forward, the traditional approach is *not* going to get us across the finish line of completing the Great Commission. Population growth alone compels us to find a more current, cutting-edge way to finish the assignment. In the next ten years, the population of the world will cross eight billion. Suliasi Kurulo of World Harvest Center in the Fiji Islands says it well: "Everything the Lord did not tell us to do, we have done; but, the very thing has told us to do, we have not done!" He commanded us to finish the Great Commission, and that's what we must do.

Even though reaching 8 billion people is just ten years away, we need to be already strategically planning how to reach 9 billion people in the next twenty years. Often, we give thought to how our organization can grow larger next year compared to past years, without giving long term thought to how our organization can add value to other organizations in order to reach untold millions with the gospel. Traditional missions helps us grow our own organization. Global missions helps us grow our organization and other organizations for the fulfillment of the Great Commission.

Let's envision the arrowhead again, this time through the global networking lens.

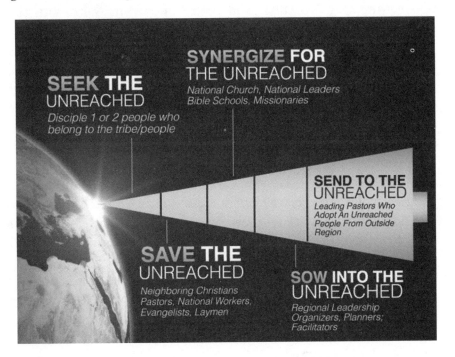

1. Seek the Unreached:

The missionary networks with one or two disciples who belong to the unreached people group.

We are to begin with the target in mind and work our way from that point. As we've already noted, there are more than 16,000 people groups throughout the world. The Lausanne Covenant of 1974 introduced into missional thinking the concept of people groups, and the significance of that viewpoint has grown steadily over the years. The old question was, "How many nations are you in?" The better question is, "How many *ethnos* (ethnics or people groups) are you in?" This is far closer to the original mindset of the first "Great Commission" spoken by our risen Lord!

Of the world's 16,000 people groups, approximately 6,000 of these are unreached or unengaged people groups. (Unengaged means that not enough gospel penetration is taking place to make a significant difference.) Pastors and leaders who are targeting these people groups should begin by thinking through clearly where they want to start, and then build from there with the globe in mind.

We must be thoughtful and intentional, using all the resources God has made available, including other Christians. In the past, we used to simply answer the missionary call and go, without ever thinking about whether or not there were Christians already in the region. It used to be that there were so few Christians and denominations in these mission fields that it really didn't matter. That mindset can be summarized by Dr. Glenn Burris, President of the Foursquare Church: "My old concept of unreached peoples was, if there was not a Foursquare church, they were unreached—no matter who else was there." Today, the Church has grown up enough to know that the Great Commission goal is better served when we take the time to ask, "Who else is there already?" If there are one or two disciples who are part of the people group, we can begin our work most effectively by networking with them.

2. Save the Unreached:
The missionary networks with Christians who live along the perimeter of the unreached people group.

Now we are getting somewhere! When we begin to realize that the Church has grown up, we can begin to move from parenting to partnering. Who else knows better how to get to the unreached people than their neighbors? I have witnessed the effectiveness of this approach time and time again in various world regions. In our Billion Soul networking summits, we ask, "How do we get from here to there? Who already lives in the region who will know what to do and how to do it?"

Of course, this model can be applied to the unreached in any area of the world. In my opinion, however, of all the dark places on the planet, Northern India is the darkest. This is where 310 of the largest unreached/unengaged people groups are found. North of Delhi, between Nepal and Pakistan, more than 400 million live without adequate witness of the gospel. Yet, over the last twenty years, Dr. Alex Abraham, founder of Operation Agape, has networked to perform an amazing work in this region. I could never imagine going into Northern India without first checking in on Alex. He knows his nation like the back of his hand. Yet, the old school of missions is still in session!

3. Synergize for the Unreached:
The missionary networks with the national leaders, Bible schools and other missionaries.

I realize that there are areas in the world where the Gospel has not penetrated. However, this does not stop us from networking with key leaders who are the closest to this region in order to build bridges in the area. In some nations, it is illegal to preach the Gospel; we *must* build networking bridges if we are ever going to finish the assignment in these regions.

In other areas, there are hundreds of unreached people groups, and every major organization is serving in some way. For example, India is filled with key leaders from various organizations. Each year Alex Abraham holds a Finish Line Summit, where leaders from numerous denominations and organizations come together to connect with key Indian leaders who represent more than 125 unreached/unengaged people groups. Over the last five years, more than 120 of the unreached people groups have been adopted by key leaders. I cannot imagine a missionary going to India with the old mindset of working only with "my tribe" to finish the Great Commission!

4. Sow into the Unreached:
The missionary networks with others throughout the region.

Now, we broaden our minds and ministry to begin to connect with others, even those outside of the target nation, to discover who else is serving in that nation. I believe the global Church is located as it is throughout the earth because our Lord led tens of thousands of leaders throughout the decades, knowing that we would need to be able to network effectively to finish the assignment. In other words, the Gospel is where it is by God-given design. The Holy Spirit has placed various groups in various locations and has now called us to connect the dots. He has called us to network among ourselves to tell the rest of the world about Christ. It is amazing what we learn from other leaders when choose to begin seeking them out and then sowing into their lives.

5. Send to the Unreached:
The missionary networks with others outside the region.

As global-minded missionaries, we choose to network even beyond the region of our calling to drive the Gospel into the world's darkest places. Along with networking at the four levels highlighted above, we choose to think even more broadly and bring the global help needed to penetrate the darkness. In the past, we just invited pastors to come; today, we ask, "Who are the best people to come help us here, in addition to the local pastors who are assisting us?"

As we research and network to find others who have similar missional interests and burdens, we gain the knowledge that we need to make wise, concrete decisions. The same Holy Spirit who leads us to specific people groups will also direct our path to others who can come alongside us to work for the greater cause.

I am firmly convinced that this Five-Point Arrowhead is the right model for missions as we move forward in the decades ahead. Whether you serve as a pastor or a leader in an organization, these five steps will work effectively and powerfully for you, as you seek to serve the Lord and help fulfill the Great Commission in our lifetime.

3

Synergizing Across the Lines

Throughout this book I have stressed the importance of synergizing across the lines of denominations and organizations in order to fulfill the Great Commission. When this synergy is not achieved, it is typically because of doctrinal differences, narrow views of the Church, tight-fisted ownership of the local churches planted, and the lack of commitment to truly fulfilling the Great Commission in our lifetime—or any lifetime for that matter.

Yet, the stark reality is that everything the Lord did not command us to do, we have done. We have built great buildings, written powerful books and music, and the list goes on and on. Yet, the very thing He told us to do, we have not done! We were commanded to make disciples in every nation. Somehow we have to get to this bottom line of synergy if we are ever going to be able to say, "Job done!"

I have watched firsthand as key leaders have developed effective, synergistic ministries in every world region. Dr. Alex Abraham, founder of Operation Agape, is one of those leaders. Through his networking over the last fifteen years, he has initiated and sustained a church planting movement across every major denominational line, resulting in 20,000 house churches! Alex has achieved this effectiveness by developing and following a seven-step model. This model is like a powerful wheel that can be rolled, when properly understood, in every region on earth. I have personally seen its success, and I recommend it to you for your prayerful consideration. On the next page is a graphic depiction of Dr. Abraham's Seven-Point Wheel.

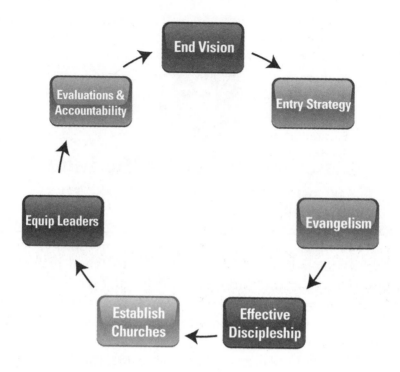

Step 1: End Vision

We are to begin with the end in mind. No target, no triumph! As we come to the realization that the weight of seven billion people is too much for any of us to shoulder alone, then we are compelled to network across as many lines as possible. Dr. Abraham's ministry is in India, where the population grows by at least 60,000 per day! Can you imagine taking ownership of such multiplication and finding a way to get ahead of this population curve? It's mind-boggling! Keeping the end in mind forces every Bible-based leader to cry for help, lest the harvest is lost.

Step 2: Entry Strategy

When approaching a new unreached/unengaged field, we should think through the best way or ways to enter it. We need to synergize with fellow leaders, seeking their input and involvement as we go in. It is best to seek counsel and strategy from the beginning, rather than jumping in and then going back later to get approval or invite partnership. If you go too fast, you go alone. If you go progressively, you take others with you. There are several biblical steps we should consider:

- Create understanding and application of Jesus' model for entering new fields
- Compare and contrast contemporary strategies with Jesus' model
- Make personal application of Jesus' instructions for entry
- Apply simple, reproducible tools for entering the new field

Dr. Abraham uses the following graphic to summarize the four kinds of fields we will enter in our ministries.

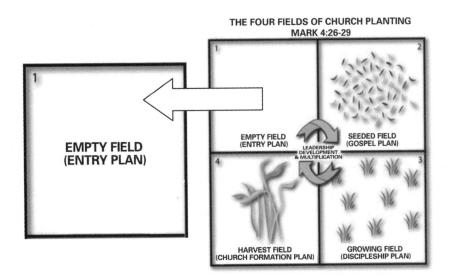

THE FOUR FIELDS OF CHURCH PLANTING
MARK 4:26-29

EMPTY FIELD
(ENTRY PLAN)

EMPTY FIELD
(ENTRY PLAN)

SEEDED FIELD
(GOSPEL PLAN)

LEADERSHIP
DEVELOPMENT
& MULTIPLICATION

HARVEST FIELD
(CHURCH FORMATION PLAN)

GROWING FIELD
(DISCIPLESHIP PLAN)

Step 3: Evangelism

The more we synergize, the more we can evangelize. The more we synergize, the more we can mobilize. Wouldn't be wonderful if we began with a plan in mind as to who was going to do what and when it was going to be done? I am not proposing that we "divide up the field" into portions among various denominational groups, who then keep to themselves. In the long run such an approach has been proven *not* to be sustainable. Yet, it *is* possible for various groups to serve together for the sake of evangelism and church planting. It takes effort, but the rewards are immeasurable!

Synergy is important not only on a denominational or organizational level, but also at the local church level. If the pastors in a particular area would take the time to sit down and strategize, they could address issues of money and assets and ownership. The key, again, is to keep the end in mind; we will give an account of stewardship during our time on the earth.

Step 4: Effective Discipleship

Today it seems that every major Christian organization has its own approach to discipleship. It is long overdue for key leaders to get together in a region or even around the world to discover the best practices for making disciples. Without effective discipleship, our efforts and energy will come to naught. What a waste of a life or ministry to serve the Lord in one generation, only to see it disappear in the next generation! History proves that after one or two or may three generations, the Church fails to continue to produce effective disciples.

Step 5: Establishing Churches

I love what Suliasi Kurulo and Alex Abraham do when it comes to establishing churches. After a person goes out to plant a church, and that church grows to a good number of members, then he or she is qualified to be ordained for ministry. Once there is lasting fruit, hands are laid upon the person to go out and plant more churches.

When crossing denominational lines, we need to have a common understanding of the following:

- What is a church?
- How do you form a church?
- What are the functions of a church?

- What are the offices of a church?
- What about headship and authority in the church?
- What are the signs of a healthy church?

A good, vigorous conversation with our networking partners about these questions is necessary at the beginning, so that there is no confusion later.

Step 6: Equipping Leaders

Once a church is planted, the goal of the church planter should be to train indigenous leaders from within the church. But, how can this goal be achieved across denominational or organizational lines?

Since we are working with Bible-based leaders, the best approach to reaching agreement and synergy is to use the biblical examples as much as possible. The mentorship of the Paul-and-Timothy model, for example, always works to get conversation and creativity going in the minds of leaders. It is critical that we have a true follow-up and follow-through plan with one another and with the local churches. Without this, we are wasting our time.

Step 7: Evaluation

When we are transparent with our fellow leaders, trust is built and synergizing becomes easier over time. We need to be willing to admit, "There is a better way than what I am doing right now." When we evaluate our life and ministry through the measures of eternity, the treasures of the temporary, and the pleasures of soul-winning, we will have greater focus for the networking journey ahead.

4

The Global Church Learning Center:
Synergistic Networking for Global Training

After networking face-to-face with more than 10,000 key Christian leaders in Billion Soul Summits in every world region, the Global Church Learning Center (www.GCLC.tv) was launched in East Asia in the spring of 2012. Upon its completion, this global curriculum will house 100 training courses from *every major world region*. Designed for pastors and leaders of all cultures who want to grow in their personal and professional ministries, all GCLC courses are tailored to be visually attractive, doctrinally-vital, interactively engaging, and able to be distributed through personal downloads and Internet streaming.

The five Global Objectives of the Global Church Learning Center curriculum represent five key points of global knowledge that are important for pastors and leaders everywhere. These Global Objectives are:

- Leadership Development
- Global Missions
- Church Planting
- Evangelism & Discipleship
- Visionary Networking

The Global Objectives are depicted in the graphic on the next page.

These five objectives bring focus to each training session. Global Church Learning Center teachers are senior pastors, top academics, and key leaders of denominations and missions organizations from every region of the world. They represent "the best going to the rest." Each one has not only great command and understanding of his or her topic, but also successful, reproducible experience to share for the benefit of the Body of Christ. Each global teacher provides wisdom, knowledge, and application from life experiences, ministry, and personal study, with the goal of providing dynamic outcomes in the lives and ministries of other pastors and leaders.

The Top Twenty Core Courses are high-priority topics essential for introducing a subject or providing a refresher study. Another twenty courses are electives that round out the core. These electives are designed with the same cutting edge methodology but continue to move pastors and leaders through higher levels of knowledge and application for powerful results.

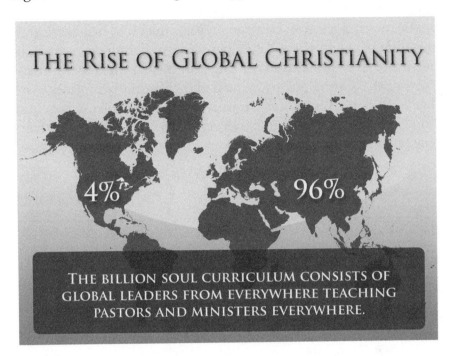

Each dynamic course is divided into fifteen sessions of six minutes each. This GCLC approach allows pastors and leaders to learn at the highest possible level. Rather than teach everything that can possibly be taught about a particular topic, each global teacher provides the essence of the most practical and important concepts in each subject area. Each person can learn at his or her own rate, without feeling pressured to finish a course as quickly as possible. Billion Soul calls this Just in Time Training!

In addition, GCLC studies are sequenced to progress in level of difficulty but are without prerequisites and can be accessed on an "as needed" basis. The graphic on page 214 depicts the intended progression.

It is expected that a high percentage of new church plantings over the next ten to fifteen years will be led by pastors who have worked through the GCLC curriculum. At the same time, Billion Soul does not compete with Bible schools, institutes, or seminaries, as the GCLC curriculum does not replace or substitute for ordination of men and women for ministry. Rather, the Global Church Learning Center synergizes with the Global HUBS of Christianity to bring the best teaching from every world region to every world region, from every pastor to every pastor.

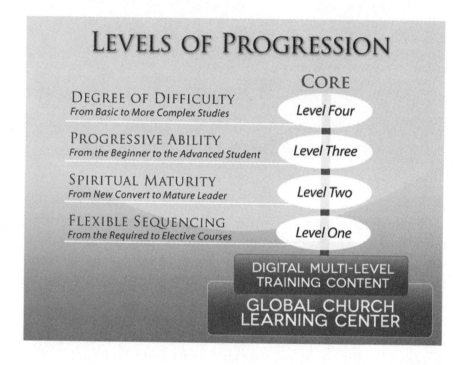

The missional philosophy behind the GCLC is that the Church has moved from *"the West going to the Rest"* to *"The Best worldwide going to the Rest worldwide."* Pastors, leaders, and their leadership teams will quickly discover that this kind of global/local teaching has never been offered before in the Body of Christ.

In addition to providing exceptional training courses, the Global Church Learning Center houses the Global Church Library, which augments these courses and is fast becoming the top international repository of the finest Christian resources in the world.

TOP FORTY COURSES

LEADERSHIP DEVELOPMENT	GLOBAL MISSIONS	CHURCH PLANTING	EVANGELISM & DISCIPLESHIP	VISIONARY NETWORKING
LDO1 - C Character Formation	GMO1 - C Funding The Mission	CPO1 - C How Do I Know I Am A Church Planter	EDO1 - C How To Share Your Faith	VNO1 - C The Essentials Of Networking
LDO2 - C The Pulpit of Proclamation	GMO2 - C Developing A Global Christian Worldview	CPO2 - C How To Plant A Church In A Village	EDO2 - C Understanding The Great Commission	VNO2 - C Developing A Synergy Plan
LDO3 - C Developing Strong Families	GMO3 - C Unreached People Groups	CPO3 - C How To Plant A Church In A Metropolitan Area	EDO3 - C Prayer & Fasting	VNO3 - C Crafting A Global Networked Church
LDO4 - C Winning My Race	GMO4 - C The Makings Of A Missional Church	CPO4 - C How To Plant A Church In A Global City	EDO4 - C How To Study The Bible	VNO4 - C Synergizing Across Denominational Lines
LDO5 - EL Becoming A Kingdom Minded Leader	GMO5 - EL Equipping Missional Teams	CPO5 - EL Selecting Your Church Planting Model	EDO5 - EL How To Study A Book of The Bible	VNO5 - EL Leading From The Middle
LDO6 - EL How To Coach a Winning Team	GMO6 - EL Understanding The Muslim World	CPO6 - EL How To Know Where To Plant A Church	EDO6 - EL Word Studies	VNO6 - EL Synergizing Across Generational Lines
LDO7 - EL The Leadership Dream	GMO7 - EL Planting Multiplication Churches Worldwide	CPO7 - EL How To Recruit A Church Planting Team	EDO7 - EL Miracles In The Life of Jesus	VNO7 - EL The Ten Elements Of A Healthy Church
LDO8 - EL How To Preach To Any Audience	GMO8 - EL Turning Members Into Missionaries	CPO8 - EL Mastering The Mission for Faith & Resources	EDO8 - EL The Gospels	VNO8 - EL How To Tie Knots

The Billion Soul Network offers the GCLC curriculum and Global Church Library resources to the Body of Christ through three levels of membership, plus a Billion Soul Scholarship. The three levels are "The Core Membership," the "Unlimited Membership," and the "Unlimited Team Membership." Billion Soul Scholarships must be applied for and reviewed, and a confirmation letter is sent to the pastor or leader.

To learn more about the Global Church Learning Center and to apply for membership, go to www.GCLC.tv or visit the Billion Soul Network website at www.billion.tv.

BIBLIOGRAPHY

Arnold, R., & Church Communication Network (CCN). (2009). *What Smart Churches Know*. Mountain View, CA: Church Communication Network.

Baber, A., & Waymon, L. (2007). *Make Your Contacts Count: Networking Know-How For Business And Career Success*. New York: AMACOM.

Baker, W. E. (1993). *Networking Smart: How to Build Relationships for Personal and Organizational Success*. New York: McGraw-Hill.

Bratton, W. J., & Tumin, Z. (2012). *Collaborate Or Perish!: Reaching Across Boundaries In A Networked World*. New York: Crown Business.

Browning, D., & Leadership Network (Dallas, Tex.). (2010). *Hybrid church: The Fusion of Intimacy and Impact*. San Francisco, CA: Jossey-Bass.

Bryson, O. J. (1990). *Networking The Kingdom: A Practical Strategy for Maximum Church Growth*. Dallas: Word Pub.

Bugbee, B. L., & Charles E. Fuller Institute of Evangelism and Church Growth. (1989). *Networking*. Pasadena, CA: The Institute.

Butler, M. (2010). *Enterprise Social Networking and Collaboration*. Martin Butler Research.

Callahan, K. L. (1999). *A New Beginning for Pastors And Congregations: Building An Excellent Match Upon Your Shared Strengths*. San Francisco: Jossey-Bass.

Campolo, A., & Main, B. (2000). *Revolution And Renewal: How Churches Are Saving Our Cities*. Louisville, KY: Westminster John Knox Press.

Castells, M. (2009). *Communication Power*. Oxford: Oxford University Press.

Catt, H., & Scudamore, P. (2000). *30 Minutes - To Improve Your Networking Skills*. London: Kogan Page.

Chabon-Berger, T., & BarCharts, Inc. (2001). *Networking for Success*. Boca Raton, FL: BarCharts, Inc.

Clark, S. B. (1972). *Building Christian Communities: Strategy for Renewing the Church*. Notre Dame, IN: Ave Maria Press.

Comunello, F., & IGI Global. (2011). *Networked Sociability and Individualism: Technology for Personal and Professional Relationships*. Hershey, Pa: IGI Global (701 E. Chocolate Avenue, Hershey, Pennsylvania, 17033, USA.

Conn, H. M. (1997). *Planting and Growing Urban Churches: From Dream to Reality*. Grand Rapids, MI: Baker Books.

Culpepper, R. F. (2011). *The Great Commission Connection.* Cleveland, TN: Pathway Press.

Darling, D. (2003). *The Networking Survival Guide: Get the Success You Want by Tapping Into the People You Know.* New York: McGraw-Hill.

Evans, D., & Bratton, S. (2012). *Social Media Marketing: An Hour a Day.* Hoboken: John Wiley & Sons.

Forret, M. L. (1995). *Networking Activities and Career Success of Managers and Professionals.* Columbia, MO: University of Missouri--Columbia.

Friesen, D. J. (2009). *Thy Kingdom Connected: What the Church Can Learn From Facebook, the Internet, and Other Networks.* Grand Rapids, MI: Baker Books.

Fuchs, Sidney E. (2012). *Get Off the Bench: Unleashing the Power of Strategic Networking Through Relationships.* Advantage Media Group.

Gilchrist, A., & Community Development Foundation (Great Britain). (2004). *The Well-Connected Community: A Networking Approach to Community Development.* Bristol: Policy Press.

Goettler, J. (2012). *The Everything Nonprofit Toolkit: The All-In-One Resource for Establishing a Nonprofit That Will Grow, Thrive, And Succeed.* Avon, Mass: Adams Media.

Grayson, C., & Baldwin, D. (2007). *Leadership Networking: Connect, Collaborate, Create.* Greensboro, N.C: Center for Creative Leadership.

Great Commission Network. (1900). *Networking Together.* Minneapolis, MN: The Great Commission Network.

Hammel, L., & Denhart, G. (2007). *Growing Local Value: How to Build Business Partnerships That Strengthen Your Community.* San Francisco, CA: Berrett-Koehler Publishers.

Hay, D. (2011). *The Social Media Survival Guide: Strategies, Tactics, and Tools for Succeeding In the Social Web.* Fresno, CA: Quill Driver Books.

Heffernan, D., & Theological Research Exchange Network. (2004). *A Manual for Networking Geographically Linked Independent Fundamental Churches Into Forming A Joint Youth Summer Camp Program.*

Hodge, C. B. (1975). *Church Growth.* Dallas, Texas: Gospel Teachers Publications.

Hoffman, R., & Casnocha, B. (2012). *The Start-Up of You.* New York: Crown Business.

Hurley, M. (1998). *Transforming Your Parish: Building a Faith Community.* Blackrock, Co. Dublin: Columba Press.

Institute of Leadership & Management (Great Britain). (2003). *Networking and Sharing Information*. Oxford: Published for the Institute of Leadership & Management by Pergamon Flexible Learning.

International Conference on Future Generation Communication and Networking, & Kim, T. (2012). *Communication and Networking*. Berlin: Springer.

Jackson, J., & Maxwell, J. C. (2003). *Pastorpreneur: Pastors And Entrepreneurs Answer The Call*. Friendswood, Tex: Baxter Press.

Jeffries, M., EIC Incorporated., & Media Partners Corporation. (2011). *The Art of Networking*. Seattle, WA: Released by Media Partners.

Kabani, S. H. (2012). *The Zen Of Social Media Marketing: An Easier Way To Build Credibility, Generate Buzz, And Increase Revenue*. Dallas, Tex: Benbella Books.

Kay, F. (2010). *Successful Networking: How to Build New Networks for Career and Company Progression*. London: Kogan Page.

Klososky, S. (2011). *Enterprise social technology: Helping Organizations Harness the Power of Social Media, Social Networking, Social Relevance*. Austin, Tex: Greenleaf Book Group Press.

Kramer, E. P. (2012). *101 Successful Networking Strategies*. Boston, MA: Course Technology Cengage Learning.

Lathrop, J. P. (2011). *Answer the Prayer Of Jesus: A Call For Biblical Unity*. Eugene, Or: Pickwick Publications.

Li, C. (2010). *Open Leadership: How Social Technology Can Transform The Way You Lead*. San Francisco: Jossey-Bass.

Linthicum, R. C., Institute on the Church in Urban-Industrial Society., Seminary Consortium for Urban Pastoral Education., Urban Academy of Chicago., Community Renewal Society (Chicago, Ill.), & Congress on Urban Ministry. (1986). *Building Strong Communities Through Networking*. Albuquerque, N.M: Hosanna.

Lynch, L. (2009). *Smart Networking: Attract a Following in Person And Online*. New York: McGraw-Hill.

Macchia, S. A. (2003). *Becoming a Healthy Church: Ten Traits of a Vital Ministry*. Grand Rapids, MI: Baker Publishing Group.

Macchia, S. A. (1999). *Becoming A Healthy Church: 10 Characteristics*. Grand Rapids, MI: Baker Books.

Mansfield, H. (2012). *Social Media For Social Good: A How-To Guide for Nonprofits*. New York: McGraw-Hill.

Maxwell, J. (2006). *The 360 Degree Leader: Developing Your Influence from Anywhere in the Organization*. Nashville: Thomas Nelson.

Miller, M. (2011). *Introduction to Social Networking.* Upper Saddle River: Prentice Hall.

Moon, Vera. (2012). *Social Networking Objectives for the Millennium and Beyond: A Guide to Developing Prosperity Partnership.* Xlibris Corp.

Moy, R., & Drew, A. (2011). *Leadership and Social Networking: Updating Your Ministry Status.* Cambridge, England: Grove Books.

Mulkey, J. B. (1986). *The Networking Of Church And Parachurch Ministry In A Local Area.*

Networking: Bridges Between Church and Community. (1984). Richmond, VA: Presbyterian School of Christian Education.

Nixon, P. (2002). *Fling Open the Doors: Giving the Church Away To The Community.* Nashville, TN: Abingdon Press.

Nour, D., & Freeway Guides. (2008). *Effective Networking: Turn Relationships Into Results!.* Los Angeles: Freeway Guides.

Okome, L. (2011). *Power of Networking with People.* S.l.: Authorhouse.

Ott, C., & Wilson, G. (2011). *Global Church Planting: Biblical Principles and Best Practices for Multiplication.* Grand Rapids, MI: Baker Academic.

Ott, S. E. (2001). *The Power of Ministry Teams: Building Community, Fostering Discipleship, Developing Leaders.* San Francisco, CA: Jossey-Bass Pfeiffer.

Partridge, K. (2011). *Social Networking.* New York: H.W. Wilson.

Paulson, H. (2002). *Global Partnerships, Networking and Nationals: The Third Paradigm in Missions.* Colorado Springs: New Hope Pub.

Powell, J. (2009). *33 Million People in the Room: How to Create, Influence, and Run a Successful Business with Social Networking.* Upper Saddle River, N.J: FT Press.

Rainie, H., & Wellman, B. (2012). *Networked: The New Social Operating System.* Cambridge, Mass: MIT Press.

Reed, J. (2012). *Get Up to Speed with Online Marketing: How to Use Websites, Blogs, Social Networking and Much More.* Upper Saddle River, N.J: FT Press.

Rice, J., Verner, A., & Christian Audio. (2009). *The Church of Facebook: How the Hyperconnected Are Redefining Community.* Escondido, CA: Christian Audio.

Robert-Ribes, J. (2012). *Connecting Forward: Advanced Networking for Executives Changing Jobs, Company, Industry or Country.* Leicester: Matador.

Robertazzi, T. G. (2012). *Basics of Computer Networking.* New York, NY: Springer.

Roberts, R. M. (2012). *Networking Fundamentals*. Tinley Park, Ill: Goodheart-Willcox CO.

Rowdon, H. H., Partnership (Organisation), & Partnership Consultation. (1994). *Churches in Partnership for Strengthening and Growth*. Carlisle: Published for Partnership by Paternoster.

Rowdon, H. H., & Partnership (Organisation). (1993). *The Strengthening, Growth and Planting of Local Churches*. Carlisle: Published for Partnership by Paternoster.

Roxburgh, A. J., Romanuk, F., & Leadership Network (Dallas, Tex.). (2006). *The Missional Leader: Equipping Your Church to Reach a Changing World*. San Francisco, CA: Jossey-Bass.

Safar, M. H., Mahdi, K. A., & IGI Global. (2012). *Social Networking and Community Behavior Modeling: Qualitative and Quantitative Measures*. Hershey, Pa: IGI Global (701 E. Chocolate Avenue, Hershey, Pennsylvania, 17033, USA.

Safko, L. (2012). *The Social Media Bible: Tactics, Tools, & Strategies for Business Success*. Hoboken, N.J: John Wiley & Sons.

Silva, M. M. (2012). *Multimedia Communications and Networking*. Boca Raton, FL: CRC Press.

Smith, G. (2006). *The Gospel And Urbanization*. Montreal, Canada: Christian Direction, Inc.

Smith, P. A. (2009). *Social Networks and Social Networking*. Bradford: Emerald Group Pub.

Snyder, H. A., & Runyon, D. V. (1986). *Foresight: 10 Major Trends That Will Dramatically Affect the Future of Christians and the Church*. Nashville: T. Nelson.

Stetzer, E., & Bird, W. (2010). *Viral Churches: Helping Church Planters Become Movement Makers*. San Francisco, CA: Jossey-Bass.

Stone, D., London, H. B., & Church Communication Network (CCN). (2009). *Pastor to Pastor: How to Avoid Becoming Another Ministry Statistic*. Mountain View, CA: Church Communication Network.

Straw, A., & Michelli, D. (2012). *Successful Networking in a Week*. London: Teach Yourself.

Swanson, E., Rusaw, R., & Leadership Network (Dallas, Tex.). (2010). *The Externally Focused Quest: Becoming the Best Church for the Community*. San Francisco, CA: Jossey-Bass.

Taylor, W. D. (1994). *Kingdom Partnerships for Synergy in Missions*. Pasadena, CA: William Carey Library.

Thumma, S., Travis, D., & Leadership Network (Dallas, Tex.). (2007). *Beyond Megachurch Myths: What We Can Learn from America's Largest Churches*. San Francisco, Calif: Jossey-Bass.

Tomberlin, J., & Bird, W. (2012). *Better Together: Making Church Mergers Work*. San Francisco, CA: Jossey-Bass.

Trevillion, S., & Trevillion, S. (1999). *Networking and Community Partnership*. Aldershot, Hants, England: Ashgate/Arena.

United Society for the Propagation of the Gospel. (1965). *Network*. London: United Society for the Propagation of the Gospel.

Voelz, J. (2012). *Follow You, Follow Me: Why Social Networking is Essential to Ministry*. Nashville: Abingdon Press.

Wagner, C. P. (1986). *Leading Your Church to Growth: The Secret of Pastor/People Partnership in Dynamic Church Growth*. Bromley: Marc Europe.

Wankel, C., Marovich, M., & Stanaityte, J. (2010). *Cutting-Edge Social Media Approaches to Business Education: Teaching With Linkedin, Facebook, Twitter, Second Life, and Blogs*. Charlotte, N.C: Information Age Pub.

Warren, R. (1995). *The Purpose Driven Church: Growth without Compromising Your Message & Mission*. Grand Rapids, MI: Zondervan Pub.

Weinberg, T. (2009). *The New Community Rules: Marketing on the Social Web*. Sebastopol, CA: O'Reilly.

Westaby, J. D. (2012). *Dynamic Network Theory: How Social Networks Influence Goal Pursuit*. Washington, DC: American Psychological Association.

Wódczak, M. (2012). *Autonomic Cooperative Networking*. New York: Springer.

Wood, G. (2006). *Going Glocal: Networking Local Churches for Worldwide Impact*. St. Charles, Ill: ChurchSmart Resources.

Yeung, R. (2012). *The New Rules of Networking: The Essential Rules and Secrets to Modern Networking*. Singapore: Marshall Cavendish Business.

ABOUT THE AUTHOR

Dr. James O. Davis founded Cutting Edge International and co-founded the Billion Soul Network, a growing coalition of more than 1,450 Christian ministries and denominations synergizing their efforts to build the premier community of pastors worldwide to help plant five million new churches for a billion soul harvest. The Billion Soul Network, with more than 475,000 churches, has become the largest pastors network in the world.

Christian leaders recognize Dr. Davis as one of the leading networkers in the Christian world. More than 50,000 pastors and leaders have attended his biannual pastors conference and leadership summits across the United States and in all major world regions. He has networked with significant leaders from different spheres such as George O. Wood, Jack Hayford, Johnny Hunt, Kenneth Ulmer, David Mohan, Reinhard Bonnke, Charles Blake, James Merritt, Leonard Sweet, Barry Black, and others.

Dr. Davis served twelve years leading 1,500 evangelists and training thousands of students for full-time evangelism as the National Evangelists Representative at the Assemblies of God world headquarters. Ministering more than 45 weeks per year for almost 30 years to an average yearly audience of 150,000 people, Dr. Davis has now traveled nearly eight million miles to minister face-to-face to more than 6 million people in more than 110 nations.

Dr. Davis earned a Doctorate in Ministry in Preaching at Trinity Evangelical Divinity School and two master's degrees from the Assemblies of God Theological Seminary. As an author and editor, he has provided: *The Pastor's Best Friend: The New Testament Evangelist; Living Like Jesus; The Preacher's Summit; Gutenberg to Google: The Twenty Indispensable Laws of Communication; What To Do When The Lights Go Out; It's a Miraculous Life!* and *Signposts On The Road To Armageddon.* With Dr. Bill Bright, he co-authored *Beyond All Limits: The Synergistic Church for a Planet in Crisis.* His quotes and articles have appeared in *Charisma, Ministry Today, The Challenge Weekly, New York Times Magazine,* and elsewhere.

Dr. Davis resides in the Orlando area with his wife, Sheri, and daughters, Olivia and Priscilla. They have two children, Jennifer and James, who reside in heaven.

James O. Davis may be invited to speak for your church or organization by contacting:

James O. Davis
P. O. Box 411605
Melbourne, Florida 32941-1605

417.861.9999
www.JamesODavis.com

MORE DYNAMIC BOOKS
by Dr. James O. Davis

How to Make Your Net Work:
Companion Workbook for Pastors and Leaders

What to Do When the Lights Go Out

The Pastor's Best Friend

Living Like Jesus

Gutenberg to Google: The Twenty Indispensable
Laws of Communication

Signposts to Armageddon: The Road to Eternity

It's a Miraculous Life!

Beyond All Limits: The Synergistic Church for a
Planet in Crisis

12 Big Ideas

The Everest Life

If this book has ministered to you, please prayerfully consider giving monthly support to Cutting Edge International at www.JamesODavis.com. Those who provide monthly support receive a FREE copy of each new book that Dr. Davis releases.

To learn more about walking with Jesus Christ, for more information about the author, or for additional resources that will strengthen your walk with Jesus Christ, please visit us online at www.JamesODavis.com.